BACKYARD PROJECTS
FOR TODAY'S HOMESTEAD

CHRIS GLEASON

BETTERWAY HOME
CINCINNATI, OHIO
www.popularwoodworking.com

READ THIS IMPORTANT SAFETY NOTICE

To prevent accidents, keep safety in mind while you work. Use the safety guards installed on power equipment; they are for your protection.

When working on power equipment, keep fingers away from saw blades, wear safety goggles to prevent injuries from flying wood chips and sawdust, wear hearing protection and consider installing a dust vacuum to reduce the amount of airborne sawdust in your woodshop.

Don't wear loose clothing, such as neckties or shirts with loose sleeves, or jewelry, such as rings, necklaces or bracelets, when working on power equipment. Tie back long hair to prevent it from getting caught in your equipment.

People who are sensitive to certain chemicals should check the chemical content of any product before using it.

Due to the variability of local conditions, construction materials, skill levels, etc., neither the author nor Popular Woodworking Books assumes any responsibility for any accidents, injuries, damages or other losses incurred resulting from the material presented in this book.

The authors and editors who compiled this book have tried to make the contents as accurate and correct as possible. Plans, illustrations, photographs and text have been carefully checked. All instructions, plans and projects should be carefully read, studied and understood before beginning construction.

Prices listed for supplies and equipment were current at the time of publication and are subject to change.

BACKYARD PROJECTS FOR TODAY'S HOMESTEAD. Copyright © 2010 by Chris Gleason. Printed and bound in China. All rights reserved. No part of this book may be reproduced in any form or by any electronic or mechanical means including information storage and retrieval systems without permission in writing from the publisher, except by a reviewer, who may quote brief passages in a review. Published by Popular Woodworking Books, an imprint of F+W Media, Inc., 4700 East Galbraith Road, Cincinnati, Ohio, 45236. (800) 289-0963 First edition.

Distributed in Canada by Fraser Direct
100 Armstrong Avenue
Georgetown, Ontario L7G 5S4
Canada

Distributed in the U.K and Europe by F+W Media International
Brunel House
Newton Abbot
Devon TQ12 4PU
England
Tel: (+44) 1626 323200
Fax: (+44) 1626 323319
E-mail: postmaster@davidandcharles.co.uk

Distributed in Australia by Capricorn Link
P.O. Box 704
Windsor, NSW 2756
Australia

Visit our Web site at www.popularwoodworking.com.

Other fine Popular Woodworking Books are available from your local bookstore or direct from the publisher.

14   13   12   11   10   5   4   3   2   1

Library of Congress Cataloging-in-Publication Data

Gleason, Chris, 1973 -
    Backyard projects for today's homestead / by Chris Gleason -- 1st ed.
        p.   cm.
    Includes index.
    ISBN-13: 978-1-4403-0555-9 (alk. paper)
    ISBN-10: 1-4403-0555-2 (alk. paper)

ACQUISITIONS EDITOR: David Thiel
SENIOR EDITOR: Jim Stack
DESIGNER: Brian Roeth
PRODUCTION COORDINATOR: Mark Griffin
PHOTOGRAPHER: Chris Gleason
ILLUSTRATOR: Jim Stack

METRIC CONVERSION CHART

to convert	to	multiply by
Inches	Centimeters	2.54
Centimeters	Inches	0.4
Feet	Centimeters	30.5
Centimeters	Feet	0.03
Yards	Meters	0.9
Meters	Yards	1.1

ABOUT THE AUTHOR

Chris Gleason has owned and operated Gleason Woodworking Studio for a decade. A self-taught craftsman, he specializes in contemporary furniture and kitchens.

With a degree in French from Vassar College in Poughkeepsie, New York, Chris had the opportunity to live and study abroad for a year in Switzerland. The mountain influence must have grabbed hold, as he now makes his home in Salt Lake City, Utah, where he mountain bikes and skis as much as possible. He is also an enthusiastic old-time banjo and fiddle player.

Chris is the author of *Built-In Furniture for the Home, Old-School Woodshop Accessories, The Complete Custom Closet, Building Real Furniture for Everyday Life* and *Kitchen Makeovers for Any Budget*.

ACKNOWLEDGEMENTS

Writing a book like this requires the time and talents of many people. I would like to thank David Thiel, Jim Stack, and Brian Roeth for bringing this project to life. Their creativity and patience have helped to produce what I hope is a genuinely fun and useful guide.

I also wish to thank my wife Michele for her behind-the-scenes role in just about everything I do.

CONTENTS

INTRODUCTION

This book is designed to help you maximize your outdoor living spaces through creative woodworking. Today's challenging economic climate has motivated many homeowners to stay in their current homes

rather than upgrade, and this has sparked a major trend in what is often called the *Don't Move: Improve!* movement. And it makes sense from every point of view. My wife and I live in a fairly small home, but by putting in a small amount of money (and a lot of time) on sprucing up our backyard, we've managed to convert a run-down lot into a veritable oasis (at least by our standards) where we now spend most of our time.

We have raised beds where we grow vegetables, a terrific shed to store bikes and more, a large deck that has been great for entertaining and a play structure that our young daughter enjoys every day. Our quality of life skyrocketed when we undertook these projects, and, even though we aren't planning on moving any time soon, we have the satisfaction of knowing that it was a financially good decision. I'm sure that we would see a good return on our modest investment if we decided to sell our house. The yard might attract more buyers than the house!

This book seeks to teach by example, so I'm presenting twenty great projects that are within reach of even novice woodworkers. Beginners will appreciate the measured drawings and step-by-step photos. More experienced craftsmen and women will find these project concepts to be a great springboard in planning and executing their own custom versions that best suit their unique situations.

Along the way, I've included information on choosing durable materials, working with reclaimed lumber, applying finishes that hold up in the toughest conditions and much more. The emphasis is on projects that are highly functional in nature: There are plenty of other resources that show you how to build decorative windmills, and the underlying theme is that the best room in your house may not be in the house at all. With some thoughtful planning and a few clever construction techniques, every property can have a functional and beautiful yard that you'll enjoy for years to come.

ADIRONDACK CHAIR

No book on outdoor woodworking would be complete if it left out the long-revered Adirondack chair. This classic piece of furniture is found in backyards and on porches all over the country, and every time I build one, I feel like I'm paying homage to a great tradition that is well worth perpetuating. As I was writing this chapter, curiosity got the best of me and I decided to do a little research into its history — I'm betting that you'll find it just as interesting as I did.

Excerpted from Wikipedia: The precursor to today's Adirondack chair was designed by Thomas Lee in 1903. He was on vacation in Westport, New York, in the heart of the Adirondack Mountains, and needed outdoor chairs for his summer home. He tested the first designs on his family. The original Adirondack chair was made with eleven pieces of wood, cut from a single board. It had a straight back and seat, which were set at a slant to sit better on the steep mountain inclines of the area. It also featured wide armrests, which became a hallmark of the Adirondack chair.

The Westport chair may have never been documented if Mr. Lee had not offered his chair design to his hunting friend Harry Bunnell. The reason Mr. Lee did this was to help Harry make some money. Turns out Harry was broke and feared he would not make it through the winter. Trying to be helpful, Lee suggested he take his chair design and build it at his home carpentry shop to sell to the locals. As it turned out, Mr. Bunnell had more in mind, seeing Lee's chair design as a way he could make a future living. After doing some planning, Bunnell took the chair design and filed for a patent on April 4, 1904. Later, on July 18, 1905, Bunnell received his patent for the chair he called the "Westport Chair". He never told his helpful friend Thomas Lee anything about applying for a patent, nor did Mr. Lee try to do anything later after he learned he received one. Bunnell became successful manufacturing and selling the chair for the next twenty-five years. He built all his Westport chairs with Hemlock or Basswood. He stamped his U.S. patent number on the backrest, painted them (a dark red-brown) or left them unpainted, and introduced several different variations (improvements you could say) over the years. His choice of Hemlock wood might seem odd because it is not a naturally durable wood nor is it considered a very suitable wood for furniture, but it was and is still readily available in the New England area. The chair never became wide spread as it never reached distribution further than a 100 square mile radius of Westport, New York. Even today, it still does not have the wide acceptance of the Adirondack chair, yet an original antique "Westport chair" that meets certain conditions can be valued at more than one thousand dollars.

Today, the Adirondack chair has evolved and can have any number of differences. Seats and backs with any number of slats, contoured or straight seats and backs, fancy curves here and there, built out of just about any wood you can think of. Different sizes and the number of legs round out today's variations, and I'm sure there are many I don't even know. However, there are still two main distinguishing hallmark characteristics of Bunnell's "Westport" chair made over 100 years ago. A true Adirondack chair has a raked, slanted back and the large broad armrests. Undoubtedly, the Adirondack chair has changed over the years, but for many it remains the truly all-American chair that has come to symbolize easy summertime living.

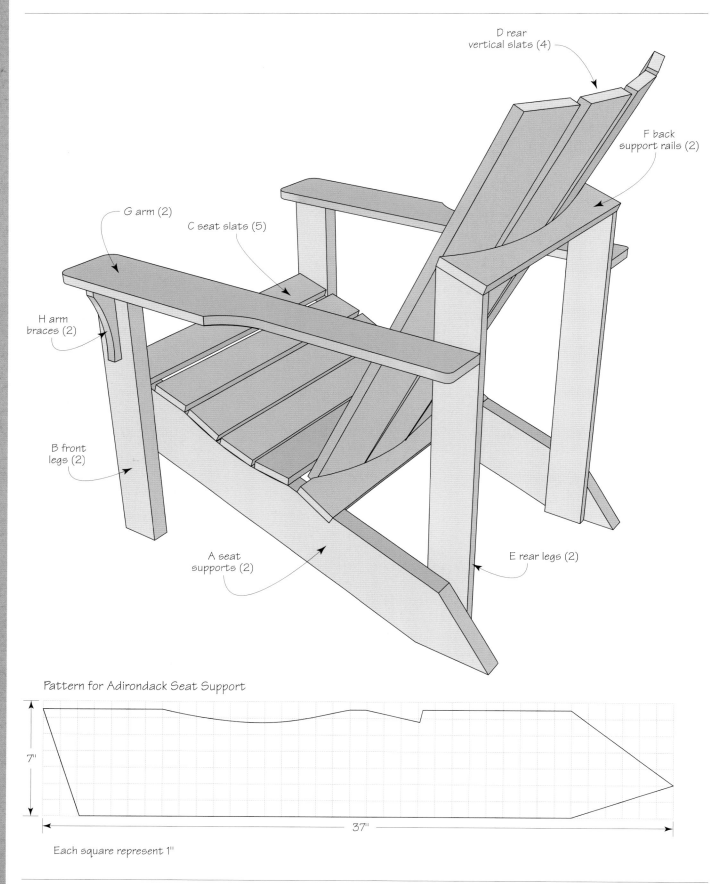

D rear
vertical slats (4)

F back
support rails (2)

G arm (2)

C seat slats (5)

H arm
braces (2)

B front
legs (2)

A seat
supports (2)

E rear legs (2)

Pattern for Adirondack Seat Support

7"

37"

Each square represent 1"

ADIRONDACK CHAIR • INCHES (MILLIMETERS)

REFERENCE	QUANTITY	PART	STOCK	THICKNESS	(mm)	WIDTH	(mm)	LENGTH	(mm)
A	2	seat supports	2×6	1½	(38)	5½	(140)	37	(991)
B	2	front legs	2×4	1½	(38)	3½	(89)	25	(635)
C	5	seat slats	1×4	¾	(19)	3½	(89)	24	(610)
D	4	rear vertical slats	1×6	¾	(19)	5½	(140)	36	(914)
E	2	rear legs	1×4	¾	(19	3½	(89)	31	(787)
F	2	back support rails	1×4	¾	(19)	3½	(89)	21	(533)
G	2	arms	1×6	¾	(19)	5½	(140)	31	(787)
H	2	arm braces	1×2	¾	(19)	1½	(38)	7	(178)

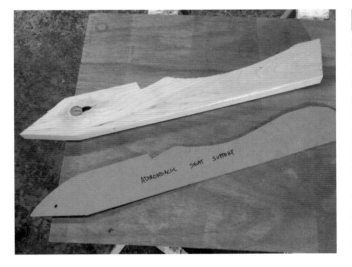

1 **(LEFT)** Building an Adirondack chair starts with the seat supports. I use 2×6 material here, as they need to beefy — most of the weight that the chair will hold ends up being transferred through these components. If you're only making one chair, you can simply cut out one support and then trace it to make the other one, but if you'll be building more than one chair, I suggest spending a few minutes to make a template of scrap ¼" plywood. I end up building at least one or two Adirondacks every summer, and it is pretty handy to just grab my template from where it hangs on the wall. In any event, I use a jigsaw to cut out the supports, although a band saw is a good choice as well. Feel free to incorporate any aesthetic modifications that you like, as indicated in the photo.

2 **(BELOW LEFT)** Once the supports have been cut out, the seat slats can be laid across them and secured with screws. Pre-drilling a clearance hole for the screws will prevent the ends of the slats from splitting.

3 The back support rail is curved to help create the fan back that is a signature part of the Adirondack's look. My method for cutting this curve is a simple one — I begin by drawing half of the curve (from the outside edge to the midpoint). Leave about one-third of the rail's width intact at the bottom of the curve.

4 | Using a band saw or jigsaw, I cut along this line and remove the excess by cutting down the middle and then using this "waste" piece as a pattern for the other half of the cut. This ensures that the entire curve is at least symmetrical.

5 | Any irregularities can be smoothed out with a belt sander or drum sanders.

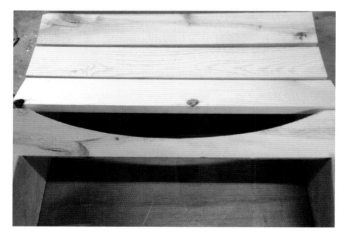

6 | **(ABOVE LEFT)** Although it is an unusual approach, I find that this approach is the fastest way for me to produce a pleasing curve on a one-off basis. This piece didn't take more than two or three minutes, and it will work just fine.

7 | **(ABOVE RIGHT)** Since I was in the mode of cutting curves, I also cut out the back support rail for the top of the back. I used the same technique, but in this case the curve extends to the ends of the slat.

8 | **(LEFT)** Here's a helpful view of the screws into the seat slats. I suggest placing the screws as far from the outside edge as possible to prevent splitting.

9 │ Once the lower part of the seat assembly is complete, the front legs can be attached. I left them longer than necessary at this point. I figured I could easily trim them down to a comfortable height when the time came. The legs should be bolted to the seat supports (flush to the front edge) with carriage bolts, but long screws will provide a fine temporary method of attachment.

10 │ The rear legs can be secured to the chair frame at this point. Hold the back edge of the leg flush to the top of the bevel at the rear of the seat support.

11 │ **(LEFT)** I screwed the upper back support rail to the tops of the rear legs, and this set the stage for me to begin laying out the fanned back slats.

12 │ **(ABOVE)** Here's another view of the progress so far.

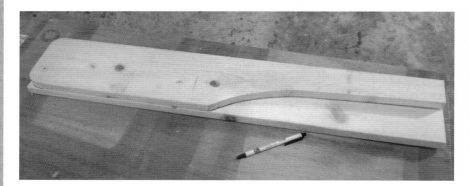

13 The sequence of events isn't too critical here — I jumped around a bit and decided to fabricate and attach the arms. In typical Adirondack fashion, they were fairly broad, and they feature a curve that tapers to a 2" width toward the back of the chair. Again, the shape can be personalized, so don't hesitate. Add radii to the front corners of the arms for comfort. Once I had cut out one, I used it as a pattern for the other arm.

14 **(ABOVE LEFT)** By sitting in the chair and holding out my arms at a comfortable height, I was able to establish an ergonomically appealing height for the front legs. I cut them to this height and attached the arms and rear legs with screws.

15 **(ABOVE RIGHT)** Laying out the slats for the back takes a bit of experimentation. How many slats should you use? How wide should they be? How do you establish the spacing? Looking at the project from a few different angles helped me to answer these questions.

16 **(RIGHT)** I ultimately decided to use four equal-sized slats for the back, and I spaced them such that they touched at the bottom and had equal gaps between them at their tops.

17 | I decided to soften the look of the back by cutting a curve onto the tops of the two outermost slats. I sketched a line to represent this.

18 | Once I cut out the curve on the top of the first slat, I used it as a pattern for the second.

19 | Cutting the curves on the tops of the two slats made a big difference — the back looks just right to me now.

20 | As both a practical and stylistic touch, I made a pair of small brackets (also known as corbels) to help support the broad arms of the Adirondack, which I was sure would loosen up a bit over time.

ADIRONDACK BENCH 2

This variation has a straight back, because it seemed to me that a single curved back or two individual curved backs (think of bucket seats in a car) wouldn't provide optimal comfort — the latter might constrain two people who want to sit close.

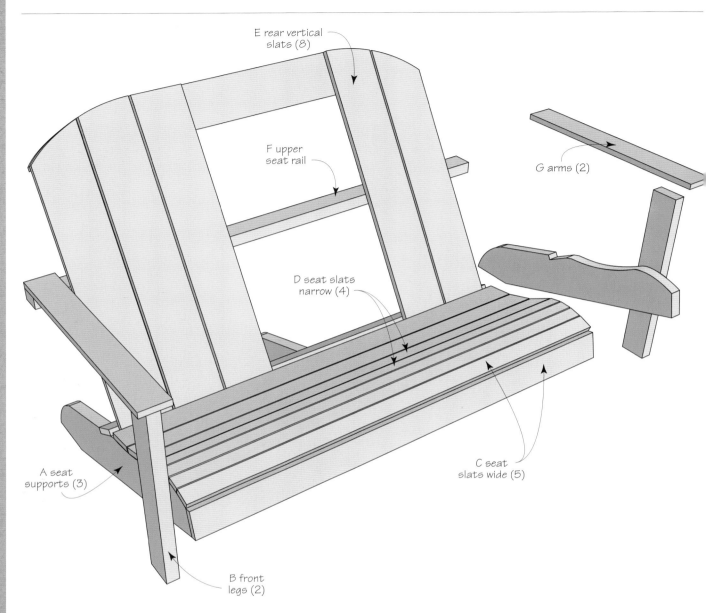

E rear vertical slats (8)

F upper seat rail

G arms (2)

D seat slats narrow (4)

A seat supports (3)

C seat slats wide (5)

B front legs (2)

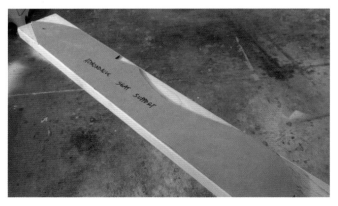

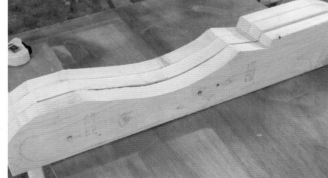

1   This is a fun variation on the classic Adirondack chair. Because it is wider, it will need a seat support in the middle, as well, so you'll need to make three instead of two.

2   The nuances of the basic pattern found on page 10 are easy to modify to suit your personal preferences. In this case, I decided to "roll" the seat slats around the front edge.

ADIRONDACK BENCH • INCHES (MILLIMETERS)

REFERENCE	QUANTITY	PART	STOCK	THICKNESS	(mm)	WIDTH	(mm)	LENGTH	(mm)
A	3	seat supports	2×6	1½	(38)	5½	(140)	39	(991)
B	2	front legs	2×4	1½	(38)	3½	(89)	25	(635)
C	5	seat slats wide	1×4	¾	(19)	3½	(89)	54	(1372)
D	4	seat slats narrow	1×4	¾	(19)	2½	(64)	54	(1372)
E	8	rear vertical slats	1×8	¾	(19)	6½	(165)	36	(914)
F	1	upper seat rail	2×4	1½	(38)	2½	(64)	60	(1524)
G	2	arms	1×4	¾	(19)	3½	(89)	28	(711)

3 | Test fit the slats and trim as necessary so they will follow the curve of the supports

4 | To avoid splitting the slats at their ends, attach them with screws inserted into predrilled screw holes.

5 | For the bench, I chose to attach the arms to the front legs right away, locating the front edge of the leg at the highest point of the seat curve.

6 | I next attached the two arms to the front legs, keeping them parallel to the seat supports. I allowed about an inch overhang at the front, and held the insides of the arms flush to the legs.

7 **(ABOVE)** As an alternate way of supporting the back slats, I joined the arms together with a long rail across the back. I held it in place with a spring clamp while I checked the alignment.

8 **(RIGHT)** When all fit well, I used four screws per side just to make sure the rail was quite securely attached.

9 **(ABOVE LEFT)** The bottom edges of the back slats will nestle snugly into the gap between the seat slats. I set a few in place to get a feel for how the whole thing would shape up.

10 **(ABOVE RIGHT)** I used a trim router to chamfer the bottom edge of the back slats ...

11 **(RIGHT)** ... this allowed them to press more deeply into the gap.

12 With all of the back slats in place, I used a French curve to lay out a curve in the upper corner of the back.

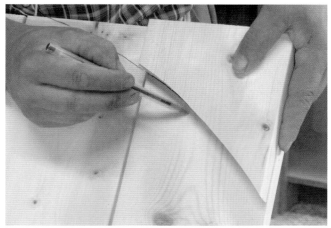

13 Once I had cut out one side, I traced the offcuts on the other side so that the two sides were consistent.

14 Any irregularities in the profile were easy to sand out with a hand-held belt sander.

15 Even though I chose the straightest lumber that I could, there were still some small deviations that were pretty evident at this point. Fortunately, there is an easy fix for this.

16 I clamped a 1x6 along the back of the bench and traced the profile of the curve.

17 Once the ends were cut on the 1x6, I clamped it in place and screwed it to the slats. This served to keep the slats flat and also to add some extra strength and rigidity to the back.

GREENE & GREENE GARDEN BENCH

3

I've included a few bench designs in this book, because more and better seating really comes in handy in backyard settings, and I've wanted to showcase a number of ways to meet

that need. This design is one of my favorites. It looks so nice that it might just be at home indoors, too.

This simple bench has almost an Asian feel, and this is understandable because I tried to work in a style that was developed by the Greene brothers, a pair of architects who are famous for their "ultimate bungalow" designs in the early 20th century. Their work is full of details that seem to be heavily influenced by their exposure to an exhibit of Asian design that they recalled seeing

early in their careers. If you are interested in their history and style, I highly recommend that you look at the work of Darrell Peart, an author, historian, and woodworker who is a true expert in this prominent American Arts and Crafts style. His book *Greene and Greene: Design Elements for the Woodshop* is a must-read.

GREENE & GREENE GARDEN BENCH • INCHES (MILLIMETERS)

REFERENCE	QUANTITY	PART	STOCK	THICKNESS	(mm)	WIDTH	(mm)	LENGTH	(mm)
A	4	top slats	2×6	1½	(38)	4¾*	(89)	54	(1372)
B	4	legs	2×4	1½	(38)	3½	(89)	17	(432)
C	2	bottom side rails	2×8	1½	(38)	6	(152)	36	(914)
D	2	bottom end rails	2×4	1½	(38)	3½	(89)	13	(330)
E	2	side stretchers	2×2	1½	(38)	1½	(38)	36	(914)
F	2	end stretchers	2×2	1½	(38)	1½	(38)	13	(330)

* 2×6s ripped to width

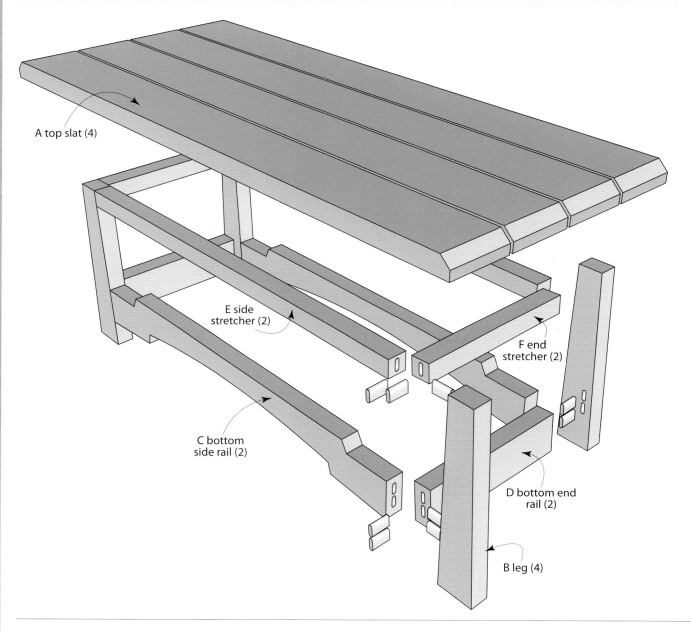

A top slat (4)

E side stretcher (2)

F end stretcher (2)

C bottom side rail (2)

D bottom end rail (2)

B leg (4)

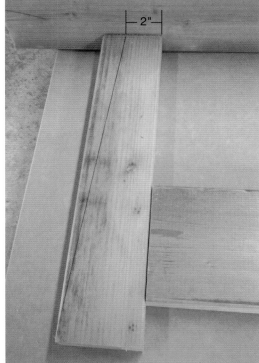

1   Because I didn't have the exact design details fully fleshed out beforehand (I was working with a general concept and set of ideas that I knew I could develop as I went along), I began by laying out the parts to get a feel for how they might look best together. I needed to determine the size of the overhang of the top, the thickness of the legs, and the placement of the lower stretcher. Sometimes these questions are easiest to answer when you can get your hands on the actual materials involved — working from a scale drawing is a very different process than designing "on the fly".

2   The taper of the legs (leaving a 2"-width at the top of the leg) is an important design consideration for this piece. I decided to taper only the outside face of the legs for aesthetic reasons, and this meant that the joinery between the rails and the legs would be what is known as right-angle joinery. If I had tapered the inside face of the legs as well, the end of the rails would have needed to be mitered, as well.

4   With the tapered leg in place, I could start to get a feel for the distinctive profile that I had in mind for the end of the rail. This detail is commonly known as a "cloud lift" and it is frequently seen in the design work of the Greene brothers.

3   The tapers can be cut in any number of ways — if you have a tapering jig, this would be a handy place to use it. For only four legs, I found it to be just as efficient to cut the tapers on my band saw and then clean up the faces with a couple of light passes on the jointer. It is also worth noting that, because there is only one taper, these legs are all the same and can be used interchangeably — they aren't in pairs, as would be the case if there were tapers on adjacent faces.

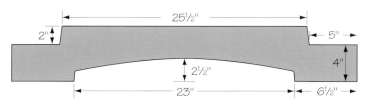

Cloud Lift Pattern

5 | Using the cloud lift pattern above, I marked the shape on one bottom side rail. I then aligned the rail so that the bottom of the rail (after cut to shape) would be 2½" up on the leg. Mark the location of the rail shape, not the rail blank. Once the excess is removed, the marks on the leg wouldn't correspond to anything!

6 | For consistency's sake, I transfer the marks from one leg to its partner on the other side of the table.

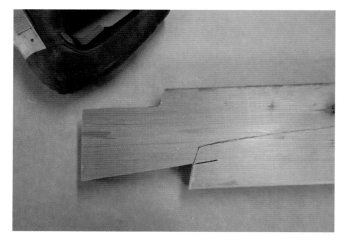

7 | I could've drawn a pattern for the cloud lift detail on scrap stock and cut it out and then traced it on the rail, but I was confident that I could employ an unusual shortcut here. I began by cutting away the excess above and below the cloud lift. Cutting cleanly along the line is essential here.

8 | I then took the scraps and placed them on the other end of the rail so that they would indicate where to draw lines on that end. If you use this method, remember to add ⅛" or so to account for the thickness of the saw blade.

9 | The rail has one more feature to lay-out and cut — an arch across the bottom which helps to lighten up the look of that component. There are many ways to lay out an arch, and here is a simple method which I use all the time. By eye, I sketched half of the arch, stopping at the midpoint of the stretcher. The goal is to simply create a smooth, pleasing arch. It doesn't have to correspond to any particular mathematical equation (it is part of a perfect ellipse). I then cut away the excess below the arch.

10 | By placing the waste piece flush with the bottom edge of the blank, I was able to transfer the profile of the arch to the other side of the blank.

11 | The center portion of the arch can be sketched in by hand — it only takes a second — and ensures that the two halves of the arch meet up gracefully in the middle.

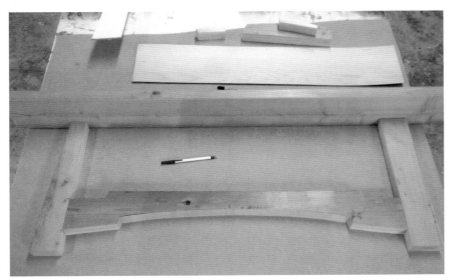

13 | The completed arch can be traced onto the blank for the second rail.

12 | As you can see, an arch created in this way can turn out quite nicely, and it is fast and easy. Since I didn't plan to build this bench a second time, I didn't really want to spend time building a pattern that I'd never use again, and this method allowed me to work very efficiently — even if it is a bit unconventional.

14 To create a strong base, I included a stretcher at the top of the bench. I didn't embellish it with any dressed-up design elements because the lower rail is already doing most of the heavy lifting in that department, and I felt that a bit of restraint here was a better choice.

15 Your method for joining the rails and stretchers to the legs will depend on your preferences and the tools that you have available. You could use dowels for this joint, for example, or biscuits would probably work too, although I would suggest tripling them up to create a lot of surface area for glue to take hold. In any event, you'll need to mark the stock accordingly.

16 I use the Domino joiner on almost a daily basis, and it is a really fast way to accurately cut loose tenon joints. A pair of Dominos will create a very strong joint in this kind of application.

17 How much glue is enough? I don't mind a little squeeze out, since it is easy to clean up if you do it right away with a wet rag, and I definitely didn't want to starve the joints. I even added a bit more inside the other mortise. And, although this might look like a lot of glue, once it was spread around evenly, there was actually very little that spilled out of the joint during clamping.

18 To clamp up the tapered assembly, I set the angled waste pieces between the legs and the clamps — this allowed the clamps to take hold without slipping or marring the legs.

19 The front and back of the bench are mirror images of each other.

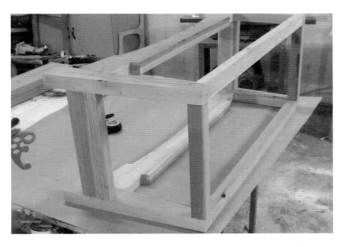

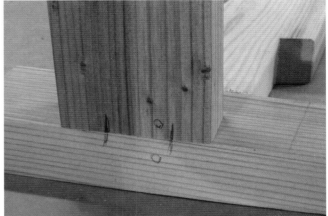

20 Once the glue was dry — at least a few hours — the clamps were removed and I began to build out the middle portion of the bench with short stretchers and rails that connect the sides.

21 I marked each joint with lines that would help me to properly align the Domino joiner, and I also made sure to label each joint so that the imminent jumble of parts would be easy to sort out. Even a simple piece like this with relatively few components can cause confusion if you don't work methodically.

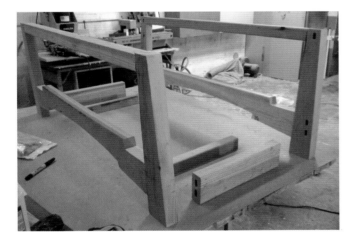

23 A pair of clamps on each side provided plenty of clamping pressure — and the tapered wedges were of course unnecessary, as the sides themselves did not taper inward (the short stretchers and rails are set at right angles to the side sub-assemblies).

22 Here's the bench with the mortises cut, just prior to the final assembly of the base. Because everything was labeled, it was a cinch to lay out the parts in the right places and in the right orientation.

24 The top consists of a row of 2×6s that I ripped to 4¾" wide to get the right overhang at the front and back of the bench. I used my miter saw to cut the end of each board at a 45° angle, leaving a ½" flat on the ends. I used some bolts as spacers to create even gaps between the boards. Because these boards are fairly narrow, and because I only used one long screw per board, wood movement can occur without any negative consequences. The gap between the boards will also facilitate any swelling that may occur in the future, too.

GARDEN BENCH

Here's a really versatile piece of furniture that would be at home in a variety of settings — when I started looking around our yard, I found at least three places where I wanted one. The construction techniques are

simple and low-tech: no table saw is required to make this bench, as it relies on dimensioned lumber (1×4s and 2×4s) straight from your local home center. You won't need a planer, either, because this kind of wood has already been surfaced at the mill. As far as tools go, you'll get by just fine with a drill, a jigsaw and a doweling jig. And long screws could be substituted for the dowels, too.

I decided to paint the bench a bright blue color so that it would stand out and lend a funky touch to the garden that it would complement. Varying the finish would change the feel of the piece quite a bit, so I suggest staining it or painting it in whatever way best enhances your landscape.

GARDEN BENCH • INCHES (MILLIMETERS)

REFERENCE	QUANTITY	PART	STOCK	THICKNESS	(mm)	WIDTH	(mm)	LENGTH	(mm)	COMMENTS
A	2	back legs	2×4	1½	(38)	3½	(89)	34	(864)	cut to shape
B	2	front legs	2×2	1½	(38)	1½	(38)	24	(610)	
C	2	bottom side stretchers	2×2	1½	(38)	1½	(38)	16½	(419)	
D	3	seat side stretchers	2×4	1½	(38)	3½	(89)	16½	(419)	cut to shape
E	6	seat slats	1×4	¾	(19)	2⅝	(89)	54	(1372)	
F	2	arms	1×3	¾	(19)	3½	(89)	22	(559)	
G	2	front & back stretcher	2×4	1½	(38)	3½	(89)	50	(1270)	
H	1	back top rail	2×4	1½	(38)	3½	(89)	50	(1270)	
J	5	back slats	1×6	¾	(19)	5½	(140)	24	(610)	trim to fit fan

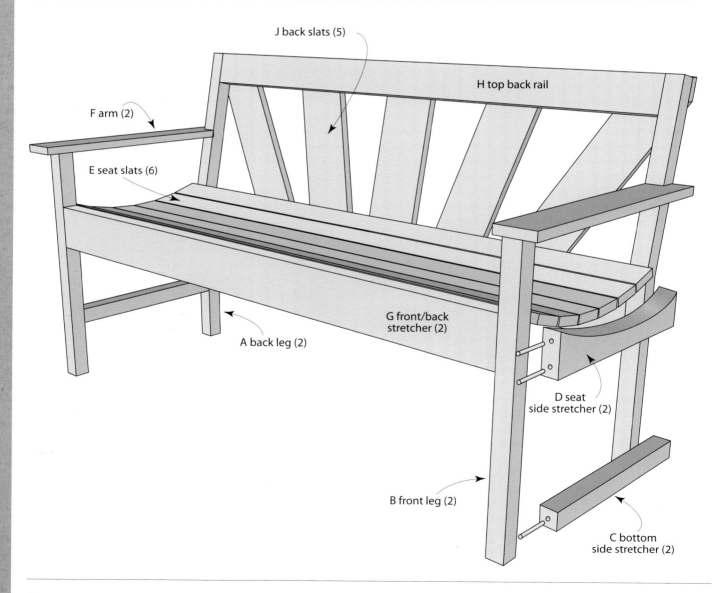

J back slats (5)

H top back rail

F arm (2)

E seat slats (6)

A back leg (2)

G front/back
stretcher (2)

D seat
side stretcher (2)

B front leg (2)

C bottom
side stretcher (2)

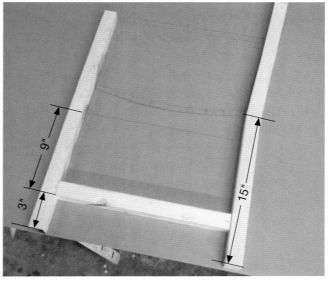

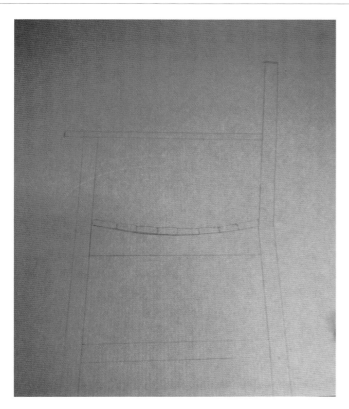

I find that the easiest way to begin a project like this is by building the sides first. To help me decide on the details of the design, I made a full-size drawing of the bench side.

1

The drawing also comes in handy as a template for laying out the pieces and marking them for the joinery that will hold them together. I was able to determine that the lower stretcher should be placed 3" up from the bottom of the leg, and that the seat stretcher is located 12" up from the floor. The drawing also let me design the angle of the back leg, with the angle starting 15" from the floor. The back leg itself is cut to shape from a 2x4. I marked 15" up from one end along the left side for the "inside" of the leg. I then drew a line up to the top right corner of the 2x4, measuring over 1½" from the right edge. Voila, an angled leg.

2

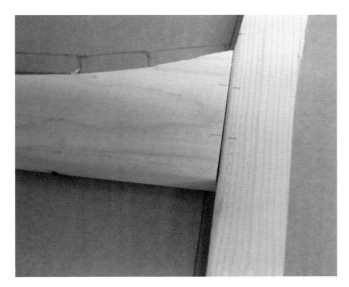

I cut the two 2x4s for the seat side stretchers down from their 3½" width to 2¾" (to allow for the thickness of the seat slats). I then marked and cut a simple arc on the top edges, leaving 1¾" at the center of the arc. I decided to join the parts of the bench together with dowels, so the marks indicate a dowel location. They also serve as handy reference points that could help to quickly and easily reposition the pieces in the correct spots in case things get shuffled around, as they often do.

3

This dowel jig is worth its weight in gold, and at $40 it is one of my favorite bang-for-your-buck tools. It automatically centers the hole across the width of the parts and accepts thick stock such as these legs and stretchers.

4

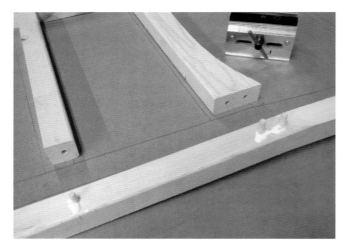

5 (ABOVE) Just before the final assembly, I dry-fit the parts to make sure they'll work. Then the joints go together with plenty of glue — more than you see in this photo — and make sure to apply adhesive to the entire dowel and the surrounding area.

6 (RIGHT) Two clamps are sufficient to ensure good, even clamping pressure.

7 (ABOVE LEFT) With the first side clamped up, the second goes together the same way — and it is usually a little bit quicker, as well, since you've just practiced it once. I like to lay the parts on top of the first side to double-check that the sides are identical and that no errors crept in the second time around.

8 (ABOVE RIGHT) Joining the sides with the seat boards helps the project really start to look good. I tack them in place with a brad nailer and then reinforce the joint with weather-resistant screws. Spacing the slats is easy since I'd already ripped them to the width indicated in the cutting list.

9 (LEFT) I put the front and back slats in first and then just set the middle ones in, maintaining small, even gaps between them all.

10 I used a 2×4 stretcher at the front of the bench to join the sides — this may be overkill, but it provides a lot of rigidity. I also added an identical one to the back of the bench.

11 The stretchers are positioned so that they're top edge is essentially flush with the seat slat closest to them. I secured the stretchers with long screws.

12 **(LEFT)** Here's a nice picture of the overall progress.

13 **(TOP)** The arms could be shaped any way you like (taking a page from Adirondack chair design, perhaps), but I kept it simple here. They do need to be notched at the back edge so that they can fit around the rear leg.

14 **(ABOVE)** I used a jig saw to cut the notch.

15 The arm can be attached to the front leg by simply screwing down through the top of the arm.

16 The back of the arm is easy to attach to the rear leg with a long, counter-bored screw.

17 (ABOVE LEFT) To provide a safe and sturdy seat, I attached a brace on the underside of the slats. The profile matches the curve on the stretchers that hold the sides together.

18 (ABOVE RIGHT) The brace can be secured through the stretchers on the front and rear of the bench. I also recommend screwing and nailing down through the top of the slats into the brace.

19 (LEFT) I decided to make a fan-back for this bench as a way of breaking up its rectilinear nature just a bit. I think it added a rather playful touch. To lay out the back slats, I started with the easy part: the center slat simply runs perpendicular to the seat slats, and it is centered across the back. Once it was in place, I laid out the next two slats by eye — in this case, that meant that they needed to touch at the bottom of the fan and they were 6" apart when measured at the bottom of the top rail. I set them down with plenty of overhang on each end of the slats so that the excess could be trimmed away.

20 To determine how much extra material to remove, I drew a line along the bottom of the fan.

21 I also drew a line across the top. The top corner of the slat on the end needed to be trimmed to a point.

22 **(ABOVE LEFT)** I didn't worry about the unevenness at the bottom of one of the slats because the back of the bench was going against a wall and so I decided not to sweat the small stuff.

23 **(ABOVE RIGHT)** The other side of the fan is laid out and trimmed in the same manner.

24 **(LEFT)** From the front, the effect is quite nice!

HOSE CADDY

5

I was really excited for this project because I think it represents an attractive take on a very practical idea. My wife and I wanted to find a better way to store the garden hose that we use almost daily during the warm

months. The home centers in my area offer a number of wind-up hose reels, but they were only available in plastic. While this may be an inoffensive material to some, it just didn't seem like it would complement the Victorian character of our 112-year-old home. My wife and I much preferred the look of wood, so this meant building one ourselves.

Constructing the caddy was pretty straightforward, but there was one functional challenge that I had to figure out:

During the design process, I quickly realized that getting the hose to wind around a roller was actually trickier than I'd thought. As long as one end of the hose is attached to the roller, it is a snap to wind up the hose, but I wasn't sure how that would work. How could you affix the hose without kinking it or otherwise gumming up the works? When I couldn't think of a solution,

I did the next best thing: I took a closer look at the plastic units that I had previously scoffed at, and I found that they solved the problem simply and elegantly. The end of the hose screws onto a fitting that runs through the center of the roller, and this fitting is attached to a swivel coupling, which allows the roller to turn unimpeded. An additional short length of hose then runs from the swivel coupling to the hose bib. The required fittings (detailed later in this chapter) were available for only a few dollars at the home center.

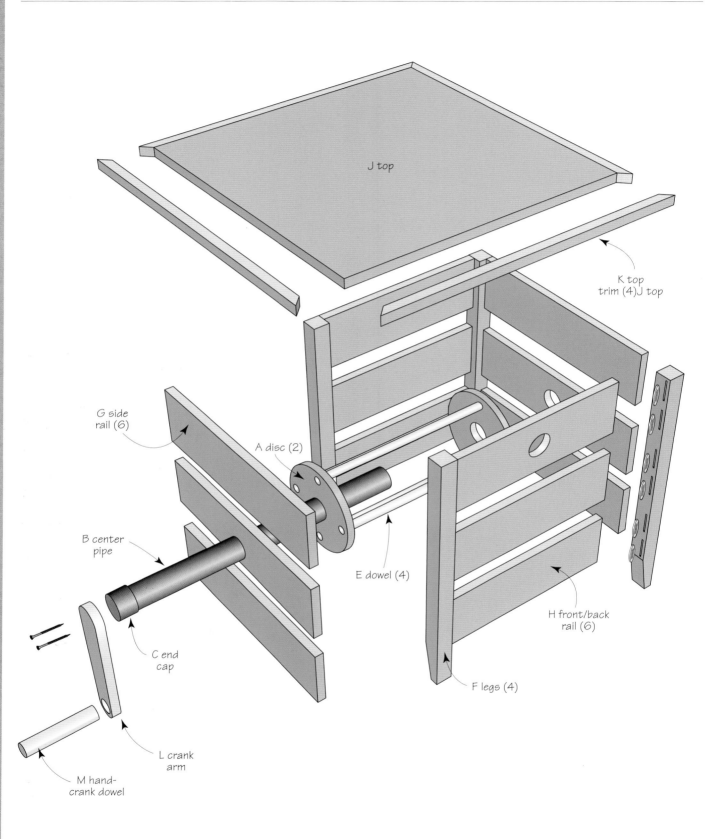

J top

K top
trim (4)J top

G side
rail (6)

A disc (2)

B center
pipe

E dowel (4)

C end
cap

H front/back
rail (6)

F legs (4)

L crank
arm

M hand-
crank dowel

HOSE CADDY • INCHES (MILLIMETERS)

REFERENCE	QUANTITY	PART	STOCK	THICKNESS	(mm)	WIDTH	(mm)	LENGTH	(mm)
A	2	discs	plywood	5/8	(16)	8 D	(203)		
B	1	center pipe	ABS plastic			2 OD	(51)	24	(610)
C	1	end cap	ABS plastic			2	(51)		
D	1	angled swivel coupling							
E	4	dowels	hardwood			3/4 D	(19)	17	(432)
F	4	legs	2×2	1 1/2	(38)	1 1/2	(38)	24	(610)
G	6	side rails	1×6	3/4	(19)	5 1/2	(140)	19	(483)
H	6	front/back rails	1×6	3/4	(19)	5 1/2	(140)	16	(406)
J	1	top	plywood	3/4	(19)	21	(533)	24	(610)
K	8LF	top trim	hardwood	1/2	(13)	3/4	(19)	cut to fit	
L	1	crank arm	1×3	3/4	(19)	2 1/2	(64)	12	(305)
M	1	hand-crank dowel	hardwood			1 1/4	(32)	6	(152)

1 **(ABOVE LEFT)** The thickness of the plywood for the discs isn't important — this might end up being a good way to use up some scraps. In any event, a compass makes quick work of laying out a matching pair of circles. The diameter probably isn't critical either — I opted for 8".

2 **(ABOVE CENTER)** I used my band saw to cut out the circles, although a jigsaw would work fine, too.

3 **(ABOVE RIGHT)** Any irregularities in the cut can be easily smoothed out with a disc or stationary belt sander. Getting the profile just right is more of an aesthetic consideration than a practical one, since the reel will work fine regardless.

4 I used a 2½" hole saw to cut the holes for the black ABS pipe to run through.

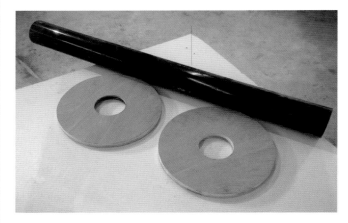

5 The pipe is 2" in diameter — that measurement refers to the inside of the pipe. You can buy a 2' long section of ABS for just a couple of dollars at most hardware stores or home centers. PVC pipe would work fine too, if you have some that you'd like to use up.

6 The hose fittings will need to run through the pipe, so I used a 1½" diameter hole saw. As long as the centering bit protrudes a good ways past the hole saw, you should have no problem making this cut, even though it is a rather unusual operation.

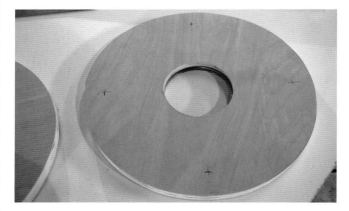

7 The plywood discs will need to be marked for a set of four holes that the dowel rods will run through. I set them in about ¾" from the edge.

8 Once one disc has been drilled, it can be used as a template for the other one. I used ¾" dowel rods, and therefore bored ¹¹⁄₁₆" holes for a tight fit.

9 The reel went together easily. Be sure to use a water-resistant glue. You may need to apply a bit of gentle force to get the dowels to seat all the way, but a tight fit is better than a sloppy one, as it will make for a more durable reel.

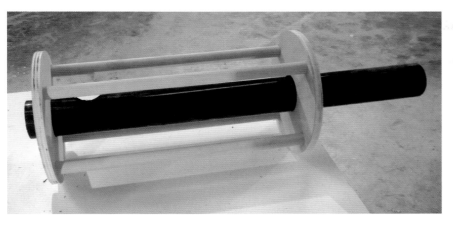

10 This photo shows the pipe before I cut it exactly to length. Since I was designing the caddy as I went, I erred on the side of caution and left it extra long until I'd finished the whole thing and could make sure that I didn't cut it too short.

11 **(ABOVE)** The caddy has four identical legs (made of pine 2×2), and I decided to cut a small taper (about 3" up) on the bottom of each leg, although this isn't necessary at all. Rather than set up a tapering jig on my table saw, I just cut them freehand on the band saw and cleaned up the cuts on my belt sander. With only four tapers to cut, this approach was speedy and effective.

12 **(LEFT)** The actual carcass of the caddy is made by attaching the legs to a set of stretchers that run perpendicular. I used reclaimed cedar 1×6s for my stretchers, and I chose to attach them to the legs with biscuits. This photo illustrates how I laid out the locations for the biscuit slots. I also made sure to label both parts at each joint to eliminate confusion later on. The slots were easy to cut with my biscuit joiner.

13 Before gluing up the side assemblies, I drilled a hole in the center stretcher to support the ABS pipe. Make sure you're working with the side (longer) rails at this point.

14 With one side assembly glued and clamped up, I began laying out another one just like it.

15 Once the glue had dried, the pairs of sides were connected by some more stretchers. I used pocket screws to make these connections, but you could use biscuits if you'd like. I opted for the pocket screws because it was rather cumbersome to layout and cut slots on the legs after they'd already been glued up into a side sub-assembly.

17 To affix the other side of the stretcher to the other side assembly (thus completing the carcass of the unit), I set the whole thing upright. Again, a single clamp was all it took to keep the parts in place while I drove the screws home.

16 Pocket screws can produce strong joints, but if you don't clamp the parts in place during assembly, I've found that the parts can shift and create small but noticeable misalignments. One clamp is usually all it takes. I recommend clamping and screwing one side at a time (here I placed the side assembly on the bench so I didn't have to fight with gravity).

18 The angled hose fitting slips into the hole in the ABS and provides a place to screw in one end of the hose.

19 The other end of the angled fitting is screwed into a swivel coupling that protrudes from the end of the ABS. This end will simply attach to a short length of hose (about four feet long) that can be screwed into the hose bib.

20 To keep the ABS pipe from moving around, I put an end cap on one end and a modified end cap on the other. As you can see here, the modified end cap is just an end cap that I cut the end out of. This saved me an additional trip to the hardware store, which probably would've been able to provide a fitting made to these specs.

21 The business end of the hose runs through a hole that I drilled in the upper stretcher on the front of the caddy.

22 **(ABOVE)** I made the top out of a piece of exterior grade plywood that I trimmed out with ¾"-thick cedar. I secured the cedar strips with glue and nails, and I mitered the corners for a neat appearance. I wanted the top to be easily removable in case I ever needed to get into the caddy. I decided to use hinges as a simple solution **(RIGHT)**.

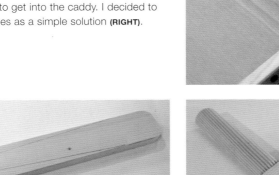

23 To wind-up the hose, I fashioned a crank arm from some extra ¾" material.

24 **(LEFT)** I used a thick dowel (1¼" diameter) for the handle of the crank, and I secured it to the crank arm with a long stainless steel screw. If the handle ever gets unduly loose, I'll pull it off and secure it with a threaded insert and a small bolt instead, but this method of attachment seems like it should work out fine.

25 The crank can be screwed directly into the ABS pipe cap on the other end of the pipe.

26 Here's a look at the nearly-completed (minus an outdoor finish) hose caddy.

MAILBOX

6

Part of my goal for this book was to come up with projects that I haven't seen anywhere else, and this is the only mailbox design that I've ever found in a woodworking book. In addition to it being a unique

type of project, I tried to create a distinctive look by designing in an Arts & Crafts inspired style. I think that it would make a nice addition to any historic home. The repetition of simple geometric motifs is a classic Arts & Crafts design element, but I did go for an updated look by mixing up the materials somewhat. Most vintage Arts & Crafts designs generally rely on a single species of wood, but I wanted to create a contrast that would add some drama, and juxtaposing a clear-coated alder panel behind the dark brown front piece did the trick. The end result, I think, pays homage to a beloved and important design tradition while expressing a contemporary sense of lightness.

MAILBOX • INCHES (MILLIMETERS)

REFERENCE	QUANTITY	PART	STOCK	THICKNESS	(mm)	WIDTH	(mm)	LENGTH	(mm)
A	1	front overlay panel	MDF	1/4	(6)	12	(305)	16	(406)
B	1	front inset panel	Alder	1/4	(6)	11 1/4	(292)	14 1/2	(375)
C	2	side panels	1×4	3/4	(19)	3 1/2	(89)	12	(305)
D	1	bottom panel	1×4	3/4	(19)	3 1/2	(89)	14 1/2	(375)
E	1	back panel	plywood	1/4	(6)	12	(305)	16	(406)
F	1	top	1×6	3/4	(19)	4 1/4	(108)	17 1/4	(438)
G	1	back cleats	hardwood	3/4	(19)	3/4	(19)	14	(356)
H	10	Miller dowels	hardwood	3/4	(19)	19 5/8	(499)	28 3/16	(716)
J	2	1 1/2" hinges	galvanized	5/8	(16)	20 3/4	(527)	37 1/4	(946)

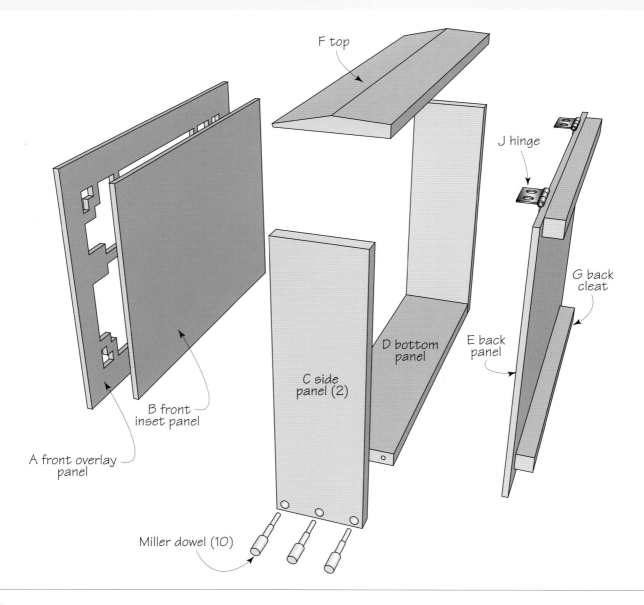

F top

J hinge

G back cleat

D bottom panel

E back panel

C side panel (2)

B front inset panel

A front overlay panel

Miller dowel (10)

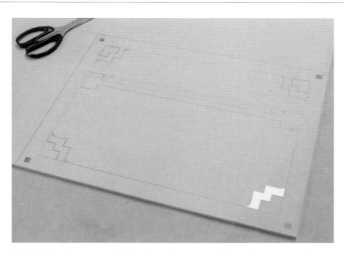

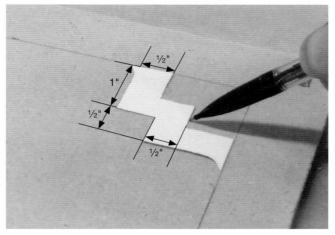

1 The character of this piece is communicated most strongly through the ornate design on its front, so that is a logical starting place. After making a couple of quick thumbnail sketches to develop the particulars of the design, I drew the profile at full-size on a piece of ¼" medium density fiberboard (MDF). I decided to use MDF because it would take paint well and it would allow me to cut out the design in one piece as this was much easier than joining the small parts together, and it didn't really have a down side.

2 The corners are dressed up with a version of the Asian bracket motif found in many Arts & Crafts designs. It is often seen in the furniture of the Greene Brothers from the early part of the 20th century. I made a simple paper template that I could move around and trace with ease.

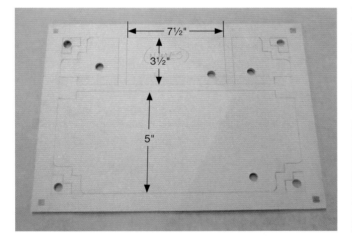

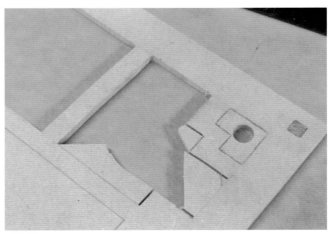

3 (ABOVE LEFT) If I owned a scroll saw, it might've been an ideal way to cut out the voids, but a jig saw with a new clean-cutting blade worked fine, too. I drilled a ½"-wide hole into each void so that I had a place to start cutting.

4 (ABOVE RIGHT) With practice, free-hand cuts like these become pretty easy. When in doubt, slow down and take your time.

5 (RIGHT) It also helps to approach some of these cut-outs in stages. As the corners are too tight to allow you to follow along the edges the whole time, you may want to make a series of "relief cuts" instead.

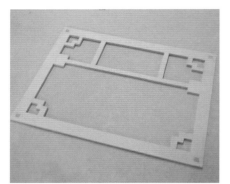

6 The finished front required only minimal sanding with 80-grit paper.

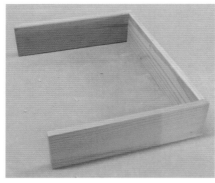

7 Structurally, the main body of the mailbox is simple: I used 3½"-wide cedar that I joined at the corners with butt joints.

8 If you're new to using the Miller Dowel, here's a shot of it in action. It is a simple yet effective system that consists of a stepped drill bit and tapered pegs that are glued into place. I like it. You could get the job done with other joinery methods, as well: pocket screws or plugged screws both come to mind as good options.

9 I decided to use Miller dowels to fasten the MDF front piece to the box as well. In this case, I let the dowels sit about ³⁄₁₆" proud of the surface. This detail is reminiscent of the Arts & Crafts tendency to embellish or call attention to the joinery in a given design. You can see small penciled-in squares in the corners of the front piece: I had originally thought about adding through-tenons in these locations, but I discarded this idea as I proceeded.

10 The back was made of ¼" plywood, which is a suitable choice because it won't expand and contract due to changes in the weather — a real concern with any project that will live outdoors. I glued and screwed it to the cedar sides and bottom.

11 The top of the mailbox has an interesting profile. I angled the blade on my table saw to cut it, although you'll note that the top isn't symmetrical (the peak is slightly offset). This shape complemented that overall mailbox design, and I created it by moving the fence to one side before making the second cut.

12 I found it easiest to attach the hinges to the underside of the top first.

13 It was then a simple matter to attach the other side of the hinges to the mailbox.

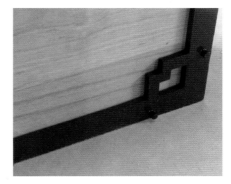

15 I used an exterior spray paint to finish the mailbox.

16 With the front piece painted and the clear-coated alder panel in place, the contrast in the materials and finishes is really nice.

14 When the lid is lifted up, it extends back beyond the thin back panel of the mailbox — for this reason, I added a pair of cleats that would push the mailbox out far enough from the wall to permit the top to open fully. The upper cleat also provided a place for the screws in the hinges to be anchored.

17 To complete the look, I surfed the internet for a free type-face that echoed the Arts & Crafts motif. If you're really obsessive, you can find fonts that are exact replicas of some historic printing styles of the era, but you'll have to pay about $20 for them. I was happy to be in the ball-park with this freebie (Vafthrudnir from www.dafont.com).

PLANTER

7

Decorative planters can add a lot to any landscape, and it goes without saying that they can be made in any style you might like. When I sat down to design a wooden planter that would fit into a *Dwell* magazine-

inspired backyard, this was what I came up with: a simple planter that can be built in an hour or less using only a chop saw, a nailer, and 1×4 material. You could modify it in any way you'd like — size is the first variable that comes to

my mind — but you might want to stick with the assembly method I've outlined, as it creates what I think is a rather distinctive corner that is reminiscent of finger joints that are often found on cabinetry and furniture.

54

PLANTER • INCHES (MILLIMETERS)

REFERENCE	QUANTITY	PART	STOCK	THICKNESS	(mm)	WIDTH	(mm)	LENGTH	(mm)
A	2	all parts*	1×4	¾	(19)	3½	(89)		

* All parts are cut to fit wtih 10° angles on the ends. Start with 8' lengths of stock and cut all parts to fit.
  The illustration gives approximate top and bottom finished dimensions of the planter.

B	4	corner cleats**	1×1	¾	(19)	¾	(19)		

**Cut to length as needed.

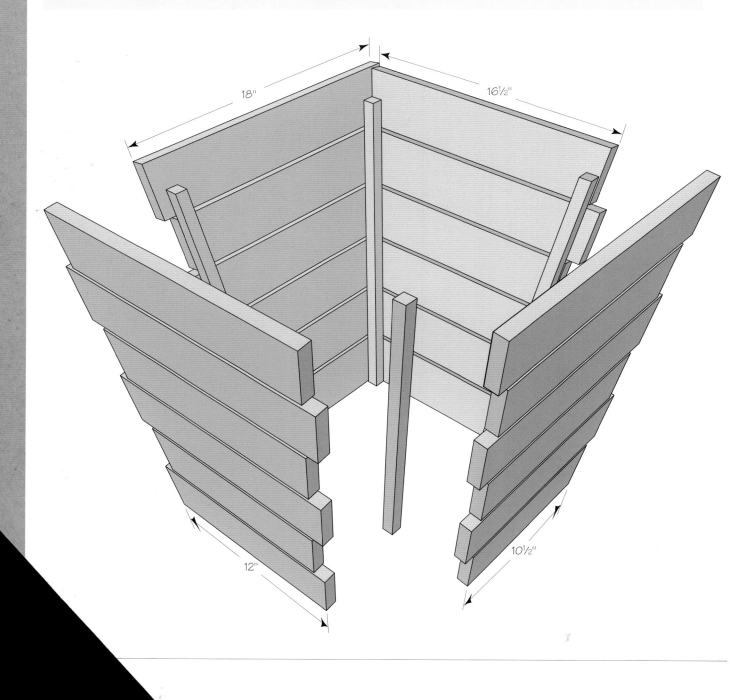

1 Building this planter is fairly straightforward, but you'll need to decide on the dimensions beforehand. I used a piece of scrap cardboard to make a template to help me figure out both the overall size and an eye-pleasing taper (10°) for the sides. A smaller, scaled drawing might work for you, but it was easier for me to move forward with a full-sized representation.

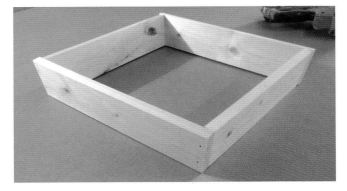

2 I made this planter out of pine 1×4s. Although pine isn't typically considered to be an ideal material for outdoor projects, it holds up fine if you finish it carefully with appropriate products. This photo shows the basic sub-assembly that will be replicated to create the planter — it is a square made of individual strips that have a 10°-angle cut on each end. Traditionally, the joints should be compound miter cuts, but in this case they are simple butt joints which are glued and nailed together. The length of the pieces needs to correspond to the size indicated by the bottom of the template.

3 The length of the pieces in the second tier can be determined by marking it off of the bottom layer.

4 **(ABOVE)** To lend strength to the assembly and to create a corner that looks good from top to bottom, I alternated the orientation of the tiers.

5 **(RIGHT)** The finished effect is kind of like looking at finger joints.

6 This close-up highlights a small disparity that I hadn't thought of initially: Because the 1×4s were placed at an angle, and their top and bottom edges weren't ripped accordingly, there is a slight gap between the tiers. I didn't consider this a fatal flaw, and I knew that the effect would be mitigated later on it the process.

7 I ripped a series of ¼"-thick shims to position between the tiers and create a uniform gap between them.

8 I used scrap redwood to make a set of strips that I secured inside the planter in the corners. Once the strips are nailed into place, the shims can be removed.

9 When one side is done, the opposite side can be shimmed and fastened in the same way. This will establish gaps all the way around that are close to uniform.The strips should also be nailed through the adjacent sides to provide extra strength and durability.

10 Becuase of butting the ends, rather than using a compound miter, you may choose to sand the corners for a more even appearance. But the fit is still plenty good without sanding.

WHEELED PLANTER BENCH   8

I spent a lot of time thinking about creative ideas for planters and benches as I was researching this book, and it eventually dawned on me to combine the two

functions into one finished product. The result, I think, is a contemporary piece that could look nice on a front porch, a deck, or any number of other spots around the yard. The design is pretty straightforward — it probably wouldn't take even a novice woodworker more than an afternoon to build — but the result is a genuinely useful piece of outdoor furniture. The casters lend a modern touch and also make it easy to move around. If you like the idea but not the look, I think that the general idea of a combination planter/bench could be executed in a variety of other styles, as well. The step-by-step photos should give you a clear view of how it went together, and you could easily piggyback on this process and customize the design as need be.

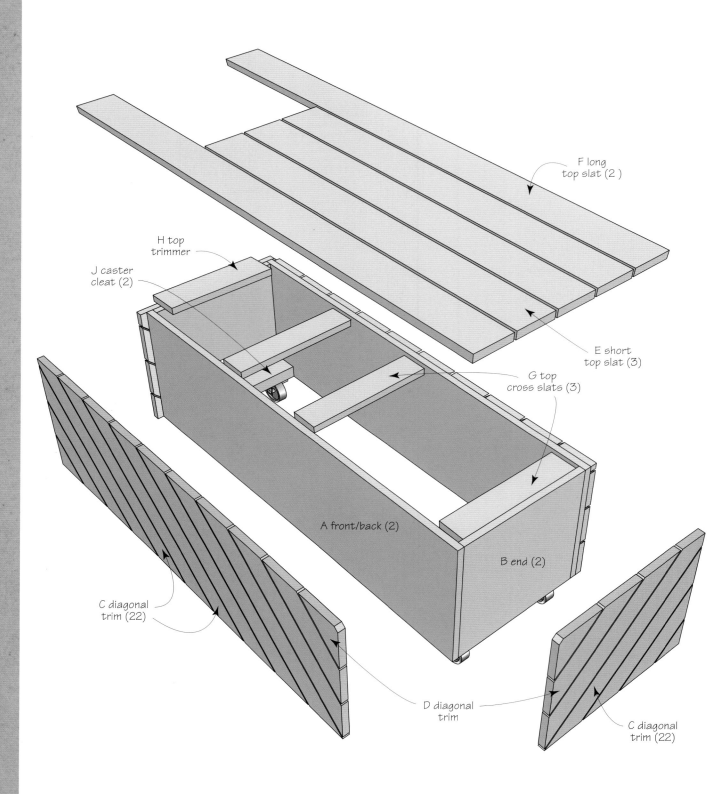

F long
top slat (2)

H top
trimmer

J caster
cleat (2)

E short
top slat (3)

G top
cross slats (3)

A front/back (2)

B end (2)

C diagonal
trim (22)

D diagonal
trim

C diagonal
trim (22)

WHEELED PLANTER BENCH • INCHES (MILLIMETERS)

REFERENCE	QUANTITY	PART	STOCK	THICKNESS	(mm)	WIDTH	(mm)	LENGTH	(mm)
A	2	front/back	plywood	3/4	(19)	15	(381)	48	(1219)
B	2	ends	plywood	3/4	(19)	15	(381)	15	(381)
C	22	diagonal trim*	1×4	3/4	(19)	3 1/2	(89)	24	(610)
D	4	diagonal trim**	1×4	3/4	(19)	3 1/2	(89)	48	(1219)
E	3	short top slats	1×4	3/4	(19)	3 1/2	(89)	36	(914)
F	2	long top slats	1×4	3/4	(19)	3 1/2	(89)	52	(1320)
G	3	top cross slats	1×4	3/4	(19)	3 1/2	(89)	14	(356)
H	1	top trimmer	1×4	3/4	(19)	3 1/2	(89)	14	(356)
J	2	caster cleats	2×4	1 1/2	(38)	3 1/2	(89)	15	(381)
K	4	3" casters							

*Diagonal trim cut to length as needed.

**Cut random-length diagonal parts from these pieces.

1 Maybe this is simply a by-product of my background as a cabinetmaker, but I conceived of this project as I do many others: that is to say, it all begins with a box that will subsequently be dressed up. I used 3/4" thick plywood for the sides of the box, because I wanted it to be really strong. The joints are tacked together with nails and then reinforced with screws. I had originally sketched a few variations which were built around a 2×4 or 2×2 frame, but I ultimately decided that plywood made the most sense in terms of strength and ease of assembly.

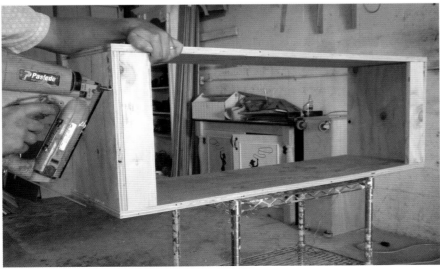

2 The bottom of the box could be made from a piece of plywood, which makes sense if you plan to use the piece for storage, but I chose to simply lay in a pair of cleats to attach the casters to.

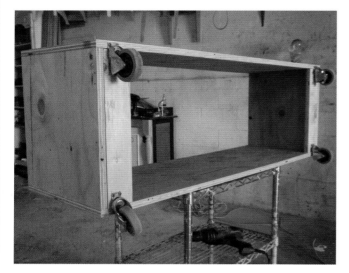

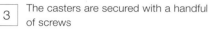

3   The casters are secured with a handful of screws

4   Laying out and cutting the angled trim is the most time-consuming part of this project, but it still doesn't have to take all that long. I decided that the trim would look nice at a 45° angle, so I cut the edge of the first board at 45°, and then placed it atop the plywood carcass. It was easy to see to what length the boards needed to be cut, and so I used my miter saw to produce a number of identical boards that could be laid out in sequence. I used a pair of rivets to create a small gap between them, and I secured the boards with brad nails.

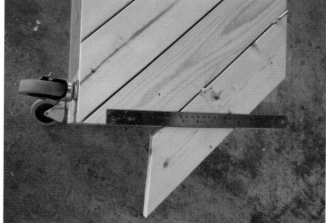

5   **(ABOVE LEFT)** Covering the front goes fairly quickly, but you eventually need to deal with the ends of the bench, which means you need to cut down long pieces. I suggest handling them one at a time. My approach was simply to draw a line on the top of the trim boards where they will need to be cut. If you stand directly above the piece and look down, it is easy to see what I mean. A trip to the miter saw will yield a piece that fits in nicely.

6   **(ABOVE RIGHT)** Feel free to use a ruler to help draw a line in the right place — you basically are just following the edge of the plywood box.

7   **(RIGHT)** A finished edge, nice and neat.

8   The other sides are trimmed out in exactly the same way.

9   Here's a glimpse at the nearly-finished box. Because the 45° angle is consistent everywhere, it is easy to line up the trim boards and "wrap" them around the corners of the plywood box.

10   The top is very simple: I laid down two long slats at the front and back, and then installed a set of three cross-slats below them. These cross-slats run from front to back, and they provide a place to anchor the middle seat slats, as well.

11   The finished top is clean and neat. After securing all of the slats to the cross-slats with brad nails, I turned the top upside down and reinforced the connections with screws. The top didn't need to be attached to the box. This means that you could use the box for storage (by adding a bottom). The small slat on the edge of the planter area was just glued and nailed to the box (it isn't part of the top's structure).

PORCH SWING

9

I've seen a number of porch swing designs that look great at first but become a bit rickety over time. This is usually due to the joints that make up the frame of the swing loosening up. Given the forces exerted

when one or two people swing back and forth, this is hardly surprising, and it almost starts to seem inevitable. I realized that the most vulnerable part of the swing is the portion of the frame that makes up the sides. It struck me that this problem could be solved in a number of ways, and one unique solution might entail constructing a frame that doesn't have joints at all. With no pivot points that could loosen up over time, the whole structure would seem likely to hold up for much longer, as long as it was finished appropriately to handle the weather.

I initially considered building a side out of ¾" plywood, as it would certainly have enough stiffness, but I wanted to present a slightly more challenging solution. Since I'm always looking for ways to incorporate laminating techniques into my projects, this seemed like a neat way to do it.

If you've never laminated parts before, now's your chance. One of my main goals for this chapter — in addition to illustrating how to build the swing, of course — is to present a comprehensive set of guidelines and tips for building bent laminations so that you can confi-

dently add this useful technique to your repertoire of design strategies.

There are a few specialized techniques that people have traditionally used to create laminations. This includes methods such as steam bending, soaking the strips in water beforehand, or using a hot pipe. Some of these techniques are particularly useful when you want to bend thicker pieces of wood or you need to form a tighter radius, and while all of these techniques have their place, it was my goal to demonstrate that cold-bending thin strips around a moderately-sized radius is actually both simple, fast and effective.

PORCH SWING • INCHES (MILLIMETERS)

REFERENCE	QUANTITY	PART	STOCK	THICKNESS	(mm)	WIDTH	(mm)	LENGTH	(mm)	COMMENTS
A	2	sides	pine	$1\frac{1}{2}$	(38)	$1\frac{1}{2}$	(38)	96	(2438)	after glueup, cut to length
B	12	seat/back slats	1×3	$\frac{3}{4}$	(19)	2	(51)	48	(1219)	rip to width

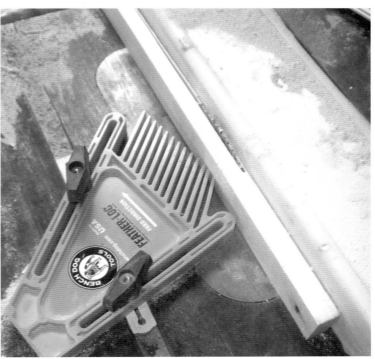

1 To create the laminations for the sides of the bench, I needed 11 strips, slightly thinner than ⅛", per side to create a 1½" thick component. I cut almost thirty strips to get 22 usable ones, and the easiest way to do this is to set the fence in where you need it and then use a couple of standard accessories to safely cut the strips (safety items removed for this photo).

2 I suggest using a featherboard to keep the workpieces from wandering and producing non-standard strips.

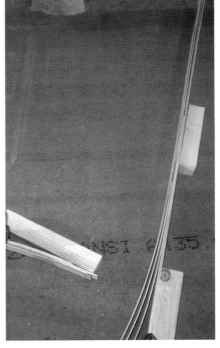

3 A sacrificial push stick is also essential equipment. My shop has an unwritten rule that all push sticks must be shaped like animals, but this humor-intensive requirement isn't necessary.

4 The strips that I used for this lamination were 8', which was about 18" longer than I needed. I simply let the excess shoot out at the top. It will be trimmed later.

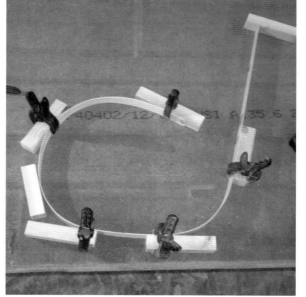

5 | The basic components required for building a laminated side for the porch swing are simple. A flat surface that is big enough to hold the side (4'×4' is more than adequate), a set of clamping blocks (scrap 2×2s or whatever is handy) and a drill and screws that will be used to fasten the blocks in place. Working from a full-sized drawing would be a good idea for a project like this, and I usually do, but in this case, the approximate shape and dimensions for the side were clear in my mind.

6 | Working with a circular diameter of about 14", I just went for it and began laying out the required contour using one of my laminating strips and a few clamping blocks. The degree to which the strips will bend without breaking will depend on their thickness, the type of wood used, the presence (or absence) of knots, and how gingerly you work.

8 | This technique results in a form that doesn't support every inch of the workpiece, but it provides excellent support on the key places in the lamination. This approach is fairly organic, and you have to pay close attention to how the strips are reacting as you lay out the blocks. You may find that in some places, you'll need to place a block right on the apogee of a curve, while other instances may require you to place blocks on either side of a curve.

7 | I secured the clamping blocks to the worksurface with screws that I drove in from the underside. I suggest working one curve at a time. As the blocks go into place, they can be used to hold the strip in position and then you can move onto the next spot that needs to be supported.

TIP You may find, once you have all of your blocks in place, that the contour of the lamination doesn't seem quite right. It may be too flat in some places or not curvy enough in others. It is a simple matter to just unscrew the required blocks and reposition them so that they push the strips into the desired shape.

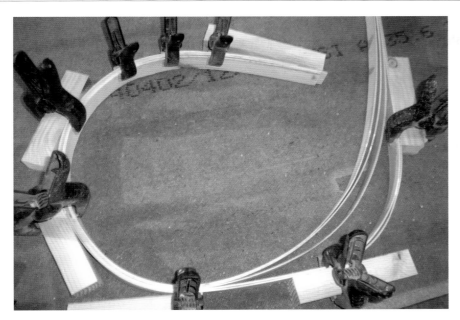

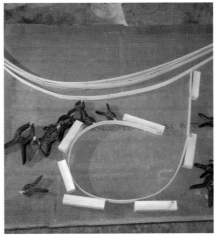

9 (ABOVE) Once you've finalized the blocks on the form, you can begin adding other strips so that they can start to bend themselves into the final shape. You'll pull them out later to apply the adhesive, but this step helps the strips start assuming their new shape and it will make the glue-up go more easily. It is also a critical way of testing the integrity of the strips — if any are going to crack (due to a knot or other problem), best to find out now.

10 (ABOVE RIGHT) When you're ready to glue up the first lamination, you can remove the strips from the form. Keping them in their exact order shouldn't matter. You can see how much the strips have already begun to conform to their new shape, even after only 15 or 20 minutes in the form.

11 (RIGHT) Applying glue to the strips goes fairly quickly — I use a disposable foam brush to make sure that all surface are coated evenly. A certain amount of glue squeeze-out is inevitable. I find that small spring clamps like this are the most convenient way to hold everything in place. I think that every shop should have a bucket full of them — they're inexpensive and very useful.

12 Some of the clamps were used to anchor the lamination to the blocks, while others served to apply pressure to the lamination alone.

13 If the finished component sticks to the worksurface, a tap with a chisel and mallet should free it. If you really overdo the glue, you could have a problem with this, so setting down wax paper or the equivalent beneath the lamination wouldn't be a bad idea.

14 For my first lamination, I glued up eight strips — mostly because I was a bit nervous and was eager to see how it would come out. This required me to add three more strips and endure a second round of waiting for glue to dry, but this wasn't critical. In fact, breaking things down like this is a good strategy if you haven't done a lot of this kind of work in the past.

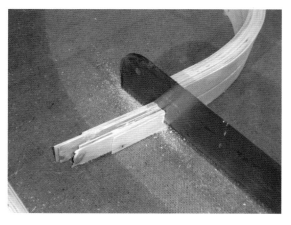

15   Because this sort of form doesn't support every bit of the lamination, there is room for variation each time it is used. I could readily imagine producing a set of parts which actually ended up being off by as much as ⅜"! To produce consistent results, I traced the contour of the lamination on the worksurface and used it as a guide to align the second set of strips. This common sense approach worked perfectly.

16   When I added the remaining three strips to complete the first lamination, I found that I could set the whole thing on the floor. This freed up the form for me to begin laying out the second side.

17   Trimming the excess on both ends of the lamination could probably be accomplished in any number of ways. I used a hand saw because it was fast and easy.

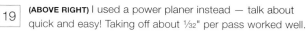

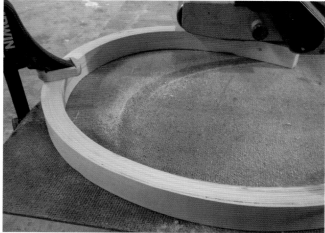

18   **(ABOVE LEFT)** People often recommend flattening the edges of the laminations on the jointer. This wasn't practical in this case because of the shape of the side, but it is an efficient method for simpler shapes.

19   **(ABOVE RIGHT)** I used a power planer instead — talk about quick and easy! Taking off about ½₂" per pass worked well.

20   **(RIGHT)** A belt sander would be a reasonable alternative if you don't have a power planer. It works just as well and almost as quickly.

21 To begin laying out the seat slats, I clamped the sides in an upright position. Even though the swing was laying on its back, it was the most definitive look yet at how the finished swing would shape up, and it helped me to see how to proceed.

22 Beginning at the top of the seat, I began screwing slats to the sides, using an extra slat as a spacer.

23 Here you can see the swing sitting upright — finally!

24 I thought a cable might be a nice complement to the clean, modern design of this swing, but you could use chain or rope, too. Either way, a pair of eye hooks will need to be installed. Cable swages can be crimped using an inexpensive tool designed for the purpose. Just squeezing them in a vise is tempting, but it may not result in a strong and durable connection.

25 (FAR LEFT) The cable attachment at the back of the swing was a little different — I inserted a hard plastic ferrule to ensure that the cable wouldn't abrade the surrounding wood.

26 (LEFT) A small metal hoop serves as a friction-free point of attachment for the cables that will connect the swing to the ceiling. I set the swing up in my shop first to see if it would work.

GATE

10

Outdoor gates are often constructed with a thick wooden frame that is covered on one side with pickets. This can look great, but it is common for gates that are built in this way to slouch (rack) over

time. The main problem is that the corner joints simply can't provide enough stiffness to keep the weight of the gate from pulling the gate downward and yanking the whole thing out of square. Sometimes this is simply unsightly, but in many cases it alters the fit of the gate so that it is unable to close properly.

Common solutions to this problem include attaching X braces to one side of the gate, or perhaps integrating some kind of metal frame or strapping. I came up with an unusual design that solves the problem of racking in a different way: I used a sheet of plywood for the core of the gate. I thought a lot about it, and I couldn't really come up with a reason not to: as long as it is properly finished and protected from the elements, the plywood will hold up fine, and it virtually guarantees a gate that won't droop as the years go by.

I wrestled with the design concept here — it would've been easy to just copy some of the standard gates that you see all over the place, but I wanted something different. Something asymmetrical, not too regular in its design. It had to be a rectangle, but I didn't want to do just a row-of-pickets or frame-and-panel approach. Ultimately, I decided to go with the sunburst look.

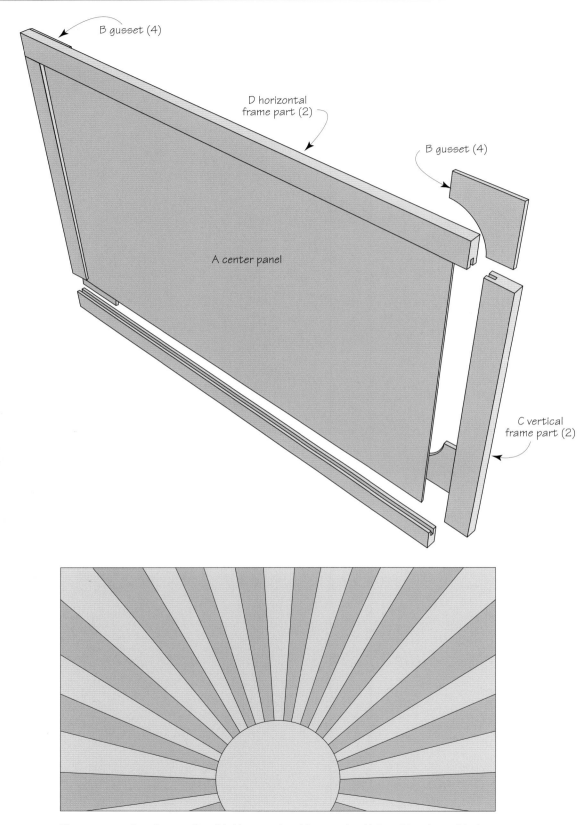

B gusset (4)

D horizontal
frame part (2)

B gusset (4)

A center panel

C vertical
frame part (2)

The sun-ray pattern is an option. My idea was to add some visual interest to a large, blank panel. Feel free to add your own design!

GATE • INCHES (MILLIMETERS)

REFERENCE	QUANTITY	PART	STOCK	THICKNESS	(mm)	WIDTH	(mm)	LENGTH	(mm)
A	1	center panel	plywood	3/8	(10)	46	(1168)	70	(1778)
B	4	blanks for gussets	plywood	1/2	(13)	9	(229)	9	(229)
C	2	vertical frame parts	2×4	1 1/2	(38)	3 1/2	(89)	75	(1905)
D	4	horizontal frame parts	2×4	1 1/2	(38)	3 1/2	(89)	40	(1016)
E	1	blank for sun	plywood	1/4	(6)	20	(508)	20	(508)
F	17	blanks for sun ray*	plywood	3/4	(19)				

*The sun rays vary in size from 48"× 8" to 12"× 3".

1 I used 3/8" plywood, as it was light weight and inexpensive. To calculate the size of the panel, I took the finished dimensions of the gate and subtracted 6" from both length and width.

2 I used my table saw to cut a 3/8" x 1/2" deep groove into one edge of each of the frame part — the plywood core will sit inside this groove. I decided to offset the groove so the front side would have a thicker amount of 2×4 exposed. I set the sunburst design on the front and needed a border that was slightly thicker.

3 I joined the corners of the frame with dowels. As long as the plywood panel is glued into its frame, it will provide the rigidity that the gate will need to prevent it from racking. You could also use a mortise and tenon joint on these corners.

4 I recommend a dry assembly before final glueup. The panel should fit snugly into the groove — not too tight and not too loose. Better to find out now than when you've got glue all over the place and things get hectic.

5 Three clamps will hold the gate together while the glue dries. I used an exterior-rated wood glue.

6 To lay out the sunburst, you could do a scale drawing, if you wish, but I find it easier to work at full scale, so I began sketching directly on the gate while I waited for the glue to dry.

7 **(ABOVE)** The design differed slightly from my original sketch. I made a few modifications to the size and placement of the sunburst pattern so that it would fit the proportions of the gate.

8 **(RIGHT)** I used a compass to rough out the size and placement of the sun. This also helped me identify the center, which came in handy when I began to draw in the rays.

9 To provide a 3-D effect, I cut out a piece of wood for every other ray. This had the added benefit of saving wood, although that wasn't the primary goal.

10 I cut out the rays one at a time based on three dimensions: Length, from the edge of the sun to the inside edge of the frame, and its width at both of these points. I added 2" to the length to give myself some wiggle room. I drew a straight line where the overlap occurred at the frame and trimmed away this excess.

11 | The rays can be secured with brads and glue. The final shape of each ray may not match the penciled-in sketch exactly but this is okay.

12 | To cut out the rays, you could use a jigsaw, band saw or table saw with a tapering jig. Any uneven edges can be cleaned up on the jointer, or with a hand-held planer. Each cut will produce an extra offcut, which can generally be used for another ray.

13 | (ABOVE LEFT) Laying out the slats for the rays takes a bit of experimentation. How many slats should you use? How wide should they be? How do you establish the spacing? Looking at the project from a few different angles helped me to answer these questions.

14 | (ABOVE RIGHT) The sun is easy to make. I used the same compass setting that I used to make my sketch to draw a circle on some scrap ¼" plywood. A bit of jigsawing cut it out and had it ready to attach.

15 | I cut a radius in the gussets so they wouldn't look "blocky" on the back of the gate. I attached them using glue and screws. These gussets reinforce the corner joints and ensure that the gate will stay square, even after hanging for a period of time.

GARDEN GATE

11

Those of us who have a dog sometimes need to block off certain portions of our yards for one reason or another — in our case, we had to come up with a way to keep our spaniel from digging in our newly planted

garden. We solved this conundrum by making a simple gate that is both functional and attractive. It only requires a small amount of materials, and if you have a couple of extra boards laying around, or scraps of the right length, you might be able to avoid a trip to the lumber yard. Even if you don't have enough odds and ends on hand, you'll only need about 6 board feet of lumber, so you can save the bulk of your materials budget for other projects. The exact size will, of course, vary depending on your situation. If the opening is narrow, you may prefer a gate with just one panel instead of two.

I suppose there is some chicken-and-egging involved with building a gate: do you wait until the support posts are set into place before you measure for the gate or do you build the gate and then position the posts accordingly? I suppose that your own answer to this judgment call will just reflect the timing and logistics of your own project, because either approach can work out just fine. In this case, the posts were in place first, so I measured the resulting opening and went to work on the gate.

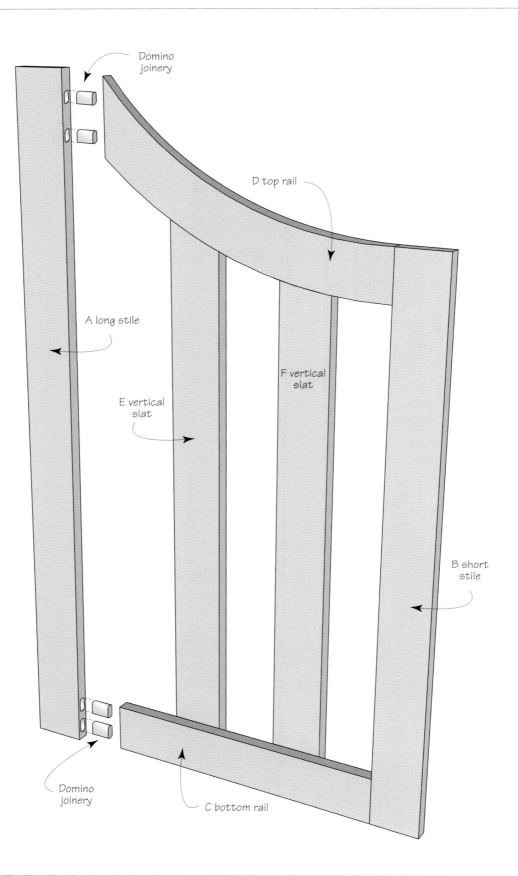

Domino
joinery

D top rail

A long stile

F vertical
slat

E vertical
slat

B short
stile

Domino
joinery

C bottom rail

GARDEN GATE • INCHES (MILLIMETERS)

REFERENCE	QUANTITY	PART	STOCK	THICKNESS	(mm)	WIDTH	(mm)	LENGTH	(mm)
A	1	long stile	1×4	3/4	(19)	3 1/2	(89)	42	(1067)
B	1	short stile	1×4	3/4	(19)	3 1/2	(89)	34	(864)
C	1	bottom rail	1×4	3/4	(19)	3 1/2	(89)	17 1/2	(445)
D	1	top rail	1×6	3/4	(19)	5 1/2	(140)	24	(610)
E	1	vertical slat	1×4	3/4	(19)	3 1/2	(89)	37	(940)
F	1	vertical slat	1×4	3/4	(19)	3 1/2	(89)	34	(864)

1   The overall height of the gate at its highest point was easy to discern, and now that both the height and the width have been determined, a full-size drawing makes it possible to establish a nice proportion for the various components.

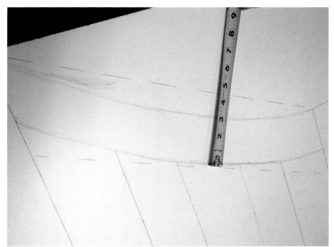

2   A full-size drawing is also useful in a situation like this because it makes it much easier to lay out the curve on the top of each half of the gate. The size and placement of the curve determines the height of the shorter vertical piece, and having this piece of information is critical. To determine the width of the stock required for the curve, I simply drew a pair of dotted parallel lines that fell just beyond the curve's outline: in this case, I found that a 4½" wide blank was sufficient.

HOW TO MEASURE FOR A TWO-PART GATE

In this case, the opening between the posts was 46½". I knew that I'd need to leave a small gap of about ¼" between the halves of the gate, and that the thickness of the hinges would take up about ³⁄₁₆" on each side, so I added up these figures. I then subtracted the total of ⅝" from the width of the opening. This gave me 45⅞", which I divided in half to arrive at the finished width of each section of the gate (22¹⁵⁄₁₆").

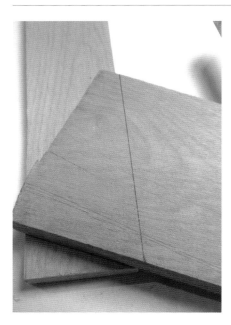

4 I don't usually worry about determining the required angle — I simply swivel the blade on my chop saw until it lines up with the pencil line on the stock.

3 Fitting the blank into place at the top of the gate is easy if you know how: my method calls for you to place the blank on top of the vertical stiles, which have been laid out in the correct position. If you then stand directly above the spot where the blank intersects the stile, you can draw a line that follows where the stile runs below the blank. (It looks like the line is off a bit in this photo, but that is just because the camera wasn't placed directly above the joint).

5 A perfect fit shouldn't take more than a couple of minutes to achieve. Once the shape and size of the curve have been established, a jigsaw or band saw will work to cut it out. I use one of the curved pieces as a pattern for creating the other one.

6 **(ABOVE)** Any eccentricities in the curve can be easily faired with sandpaper and a rasp. I often use a belt sander to tackle the outside portion of the curve and a sanding drum mounted on a drill press for the inside of the curve. Your approach here would naturally be dictated by the tools that you have available.

7 **(RIGHT)** The final result looks quite nice.

8 I built the frames for the gate using pretty standard techniques: in this case, I used Dominoes to join the stiles to the rails, but you could also use dowels or anything else that you're comfortable with — just make sure to use an adhesive that is rated for outdoor use.

9 After the glue has had time to dry, the slats can be attached to the frame. I had decided early on in the design process that I wanted the slats to be attached to the back side of the gate because I liked the way this provide more visual depth to the gate than setting them inside the frame. This is a small difference and it is simply a matter of what one finds aesthetically pleasing than anything else.

10 (ABOVE LEFT) If you prefer the slats to be inset between the top and bottom rails, you would need to take care of this prior to assembling the gate's outer frame. Dowels or Dominos would be a good option here.

11 (ABOVE RIGHT) Hanging the gate is a fairly simply matter as long as the posts are plumb. The exact method you use will depend on the type of hinges that you have.

12 (RIGHT) This latch holds the gates closed as well as keeping the gates in line with each other.

PERGOLA

Pergolas offer one of the most effective ways that I know to enhance an outdoor space while using a fairly small amount of materials. A simple frame — the slightest hint of a roof and walls — can define an

outdoor room and set the stage for all kinds of backyard fun. It can also help a bland deck feel much more finished.

My clients have put a lot of work into sprucing up their yard over the past few years, and the need to embellish the deck became a more pressing issue as time went on. That tends to be the problem with home improvement — when one thing has been

visibly improved, your attention naturally drifts to other things that suddenly look worse by comparison. In this case, some type of additional structure was required to liven up the transition from the house to the yard — a pergola was a natural choice.

We debated the use of beefier framing members, but 4×4s ended up feeling like a reasonable choice.

We had considered the idea of livening up the design with an unusual roof structure — something gabled, which seemed like a neat variation on the typical flat roof of a pergola but we ultimately rejected this idea as we didn't have enough height to work with to make the gable high enough to look right. A minor variation that we did proceed with was to use only a single layer of rafters instead of the double-layer set at right angles to each other. This simpler arrangement looked great, and a second layer of rafters wouldn't have added much, in our opinion.

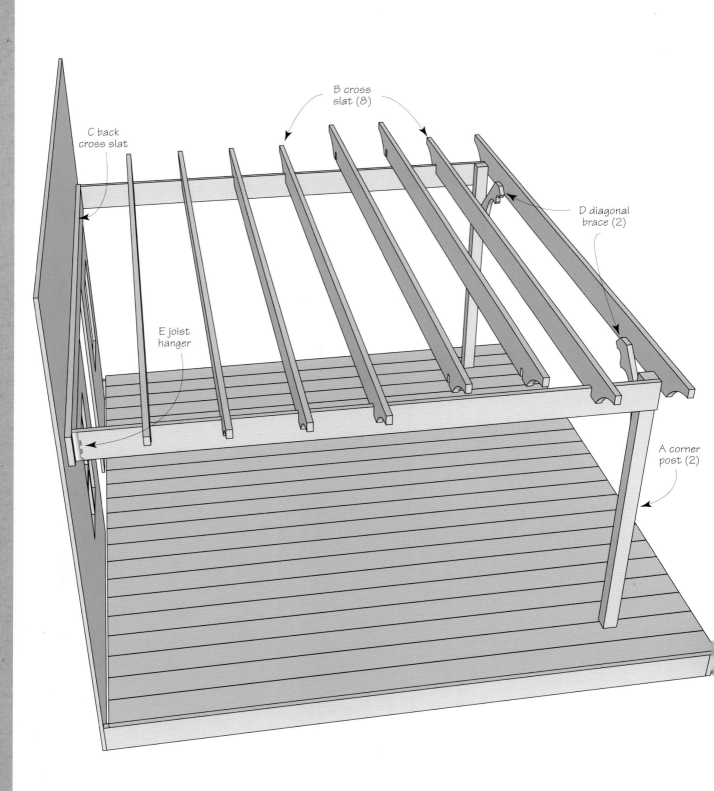

B cross
slat (8)

C back
cross slat

D diagonal
brace (2)

E joist
hanger

A corner
post (2)

PERGOLA • INCHES (MILLIMETERS)

REFERENCE	QUANTITY	PART	STOCK	THICKNESS	(mm)	WIDTH	(mm)	LENGTH	(mm)
A	4	corner posts	4×4	3½	(89)	3½	(89)	96	(2438)
B	8	cross slats	2×6	1½	(38)	5½	(140)	14'	(4.27m)
C	1	back cross slat	2×8	1½	(38)	7½	(191)	14'	(4.27m)
D	2	diagonal braces	2×8	1½	(38)	7½	(38)	36	(914)
E	2	Simpson (or similar) joist hangers for 2×6s							

BUILD IT STRONG To build the strongest possible structure, I was adamant about making sure that the material used in all of the long spans was made out of single pieces. It would've been easier to work with shorter lengths, especially since I was working alone, but reducing the number of joints was pretty critical to being able to bridge the long (14') spans that we required. The actual dimensions of your own project will of course dictate the materials that you end up using, but this strategy may help you, as well.

1 **(TOP LEFT)** One of the most challenging parts of the job was actually just getting the material to the job site. The final dimensions of the pergola required that we use 14' long lumber, and that is considerably longer than I'm used to. My trusty van was up for the job, and I felt fine about it since I only had to go about a mile, but use your judgment and make sure you find a safe way to transport the materials if you need to use unusually long stock.

2 **(BOTTOM LEFT)** These homeowners had always felt (for good reason!) that this spot was just crying out for a pergola or something like it. The deck is large enough for entertaining but didn't add a lot in the way of style or ambiance. And, being avid gardeners, they were eager to use the pergola as a support for growing grapes, which will certainly add a lot of character to the space come spring.

3 The location of the electrical panel didn't really pose a problem, but it was a consideration. The conduit that supplies the house with power was positioned right where I had hoped to attach the pergola to the house. This wasn't a concern in the end, as I simply shortened the width of the pergola by about 6".

4 Anchoring the components to the deck and the wall of the house is easily accomplished using exterior-grade galvanized fasteners that are designed for the job. Properly attached, these parts will last for the life of the pergola and then some.

5 **(ABOVE LEFT)** The first piece to set in place is the ledger board that will anchor the structure to the exterior wall of the home. To hold it in place, I angled two 4×4 posts at the correct height. Even if you're stuck working alone, this method is easy and safe, as long as you work slowly and with care.

6 **(ABOVE RIGHT)** While it was temporarily supported by the 4×4s, I used a level to confirm the exact position of the ledger board. I had gotten close. Only one of the 4×4s had to go up ¼", which was a simple adjustment.

7 **(RIGHT)** Once it had been leveled, I predrilled the ledger board to accept a series of 4" long screws to hold it to the sheathing behind the stucco (I reinforced this connection later with 6" lag bolts into the studs, but this held it in place temporarily and allowed me to remove the 4×4 supports).

8 My wish list includes a cordless impact driver, but in the meantime, I manage just fine when it comes time to drive long screws. The socket-type head helps, as there is no chance of slipping or stripping.

9 The ledger board in place. Getting it set provided me with a known height that I could use to set the height and position of the support posts.

10 (ABOVE LEFT) Establishing the location for one of the corner posts came next. I anchored it to the deck as per the manufacturer's instructions (Don't skimp on screws. Code usually requires you to use all of the screw holes anyway). Note that I anchored this post in place prior to cutting it to length: The strategy here is to install a post that is longer than necessary and cut back the excess once you've figured out the correct height.

11 (ABOVE RIGHT) To determine the height, it is essential to run a level line from the top of the ledger board. Because they don't make 14'-long levels, and they'd be unwieldy if they did exist, I resorted to the centuries-old string level. I fastened the string in place on the 'fixed' end by looping it around a screw.

12 (LEFT) The other end of the string is the loose end. Pull it tight across the span and raise or lower it until the bubble is centered. The post can then be marked where the string intersects it. I temporarily fastened this end to a screw, just to make things easier.

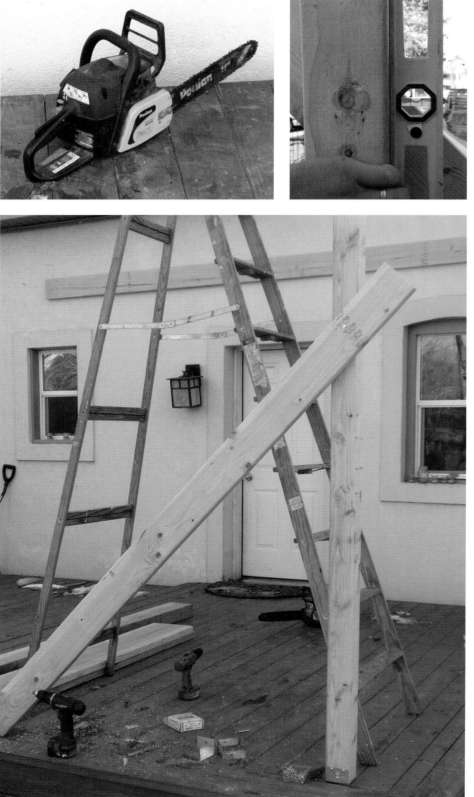

13 **(FAR LEFT)** This may earn me some complaints from the purists, but I find that a chainsaw is a reasonable way to cut 4×4s in the field. The stock is too wide for a circular saw or jigsaw, and most sawzall blades deflect and produce a sloppy cut.

14 **(LEFT)** Before connecting the crosspieces to the posts, you'll want to use a level to ensure that they're plumb.

16 The crosspieces that connect the ledger board to the corner posts are supported by standard joist hangers, which are simply screwed on.

17 One person can easily lift the cross-pieces if one end is set into the joist hanger as a pivot point.

15 Diagonal braces are a simple, yet effective, way to hold the posts in place once they've been determined to be plumb.

18 The other end of the crosspiece can be held by a clamp. Because you've already established that the top of the post is level with the top of the ledger, you should be able to just align the crosspiece accordingly, but I suggest double-checking this with a level. The crosspiece can then be secured with long screws.

19 The excess can be trimmed off with a jigsaw.

21 **(LEFT)** I decided to reinforce the long span on the sides of the pergola with a pair of extra posts. I set the post base halfway between the corner of the deck and the wall of the house.

20 Once the other corner post and crosspiece have been assembled in the same way, you can attach the front crosspiece. I used a bar clamp to provide a temporary perch for one end of the cross piece while I lifted the other end.

22 **(ABOVE)** This pergola derives a lot of strength and character from the curvy corner braces that help reinforce the joint between the posts and the crosspieces. After experimenting a bit, I came up with a profile that I liked and used it as a template for the others. I lopped off the two corners at 45° angles, cutting 7" in from the left, and 3" in from the right. A 4" diameter arc was cut on the right, 2" from the end. The larger arc was simply drawn freehand, extending in on the piece and stopping 3" from the opposite edge.

23   I came up with a couple of different brace designs that I liked, and I put up one of each so my clients could choose their favorite. This one featured a small corner drop at the top which is very much in the character of their Victorian home.

24   This one is a bit cleaner and would be appropriate for a home of most any vintage.

25   The rafters that span the crosspieces make a big impact in terms of creating the feeling that the deck is indeed an outdoor room. We spaced them 18" apart, and each one required a bit of jigsaw work on the ends. After creating the first, I made a pattern and the rest of this part of the job went fairly quickly.

26   The curved cutout on the ends of the rafters is a traditional detail on many pergola designs. It provides a nice relief in what is otherwise a pretty rectilinear structure, and adds a cool detail for the eye to hone in on.

27   I had originally imagined built-in benches along the edges of the deck, but it occurred to me that free-standing benches would work just as well — maybe even better. This simple bench design is sturdy and offers the flexibility to position the benches anywhere; maybe even down in the grass to seat guests around a bonfire.

28   I used 3½" exterior-grade screws to put the benches together. Because the grain orientation is the same on the end panels as it is in the top, screws can be driven down through the top without raising concerns about wood movement causing problems later on.

29 The finished benches are simple, sturdy and adaptable to any number of settings.

30 My clients had already thought about how they would use the pergola long before I arrived to help build it. For the next growing season, they knew they'd need a large planter where they could grow grapes or climbing vines.

BUILDING THE PLANTER

1 **(LEFT)** To keep the cost down and provide a sturdy and durable end product, I used 2×4s as legs. With a dado blade in the table saw, I milled a ¾"-deep groove on the narrow edge of each leg.

2 **(BELOW LEFT)** Without moving the fence, I cut a groove into the wide side of the 2×4s as well. These grooves will house the side panels.

3 **(BELOW RIGHT)** Since the dado blade was all set up, I ripped a groove in two lengths of 2×4 that I had planned to use to trim out the top of the planter.

BUILDING THE PLANTER (CONTINUED)

4 **(LEFT)** The side panels were made from ½" plywood ripped into 12" widths.

5 **(ABOVE)** By pushing the leg and side panel together, I was able to decide about a curved shape for the bottom portion of the leg. This curved element is reminiscent of the cut on the ends of the pergola's rafters.

6 **(ABOVE)** Once one leg was cut out, it worked as a template for the other legs.

7 **(RIGHT)** Here's an important tip any time that you're making a table, bench, planter or anything else with legs: Make sure you work in pairs. Each end of the planter requires a "right" and "left" side, which are mirror images of each other. You'll need two of each for the whole project.

9 I used an exterior-grade construction adhesive. It takes a while to set up but provides a strong, water-resistant bond.

8 Note that the top of the side panel protrudes ¾" above the leg. This will provide a means of attaching the 2×4 trim to the top.

10 **(ABOVE)** I reinforced the joint with screws on the inside.

11 **(RIGHT)** Adding the shorter side panels created a U-shaped subassembly that allowed me to go one step-at-a-time. I didn't have to rush to get everything put together all at once, which can be stressful, messy and problematic!

12 **(LEFT)** After assembling the other long side, I attached it to the rest of the planter.

13 **(ABOVE)** The mitered trim didn't need to be measured. I marked the necessary lengths using the assembly and cut them to fit.

15 My plan for this planter was that it would be used to hold a plastic or metal planting tub, or perhaps a set of pots. To hold these items off the ground, I attached a series of 2×4s across the bottom between the long side panels. They could be covered with a piece of scrap plywood to provide plenty of support.

14 Adhesive on the miter joints and along the dado joint is a necessity.

PLAYHOUSE

13

When our young daughter became old enough to get some use out of a playhouse, I began the process by looking online to get some ideas. What I found convinced me more than ever that I'd be building it myself

— nice playhouses can easily cost thousands of dollars — and I quickly saw that building it myself represented not only a chance to get exactly what I wanted but also an opportunity to save a ton of money. The finished version that I ended up building in less than a day cost about $150 and is a perfect fit for our backyard in terms of size, style and features.

I decided to incorporate a deck into the house, but even if you don't decided to go this route, the construction techniques described here will still be useful.

Our ideal site for the playhouse didn't happen to be flat, but this is no reason to rule it out. Building on a slope is kid stuff when you know how.

In terms of style, the sky is the limit: Some people choose a theme (i.e. castle, or rustic fort) but we just went for a fairly neutral look that could lend itself to whatever imaginary whims might arise. I have a hunch that most of the

attention to the visual aspects of the design are more for the adults than the kids, anyway.

In terms of logistics, you may be wondering if you'll need to get a building inspector involved. The answer is probably not — most municipalities exempt structures smaller than 120 square feet from their permitting and inspection processes. It never hurts to double check. You'll probably be able to find the info you need on the internet.

I chose not to set the base in concrete, since our soil is quite hard in the high desert where we make our home, and the loads placed on the supports posts are pretty modest, but if you're interested, I do discuss methods for setting posts in concrete in another section of this book. Pre-cast concrete post bases would also be a quick and effective way to go.

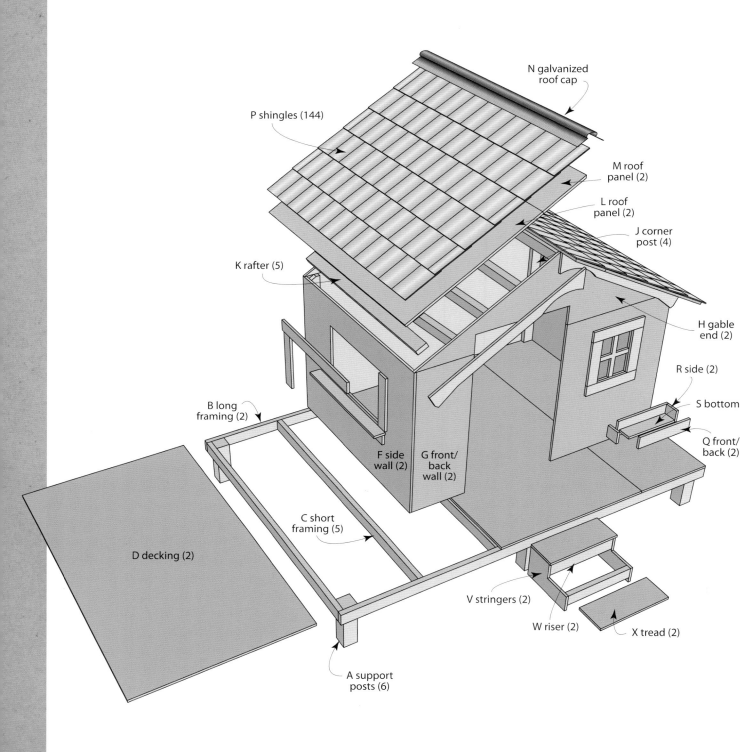

N galvanized roof cap

P shingles (144)

M roof panel (2)

L roof panel (2)

J corner post (4)

K rafter (5)

H gable end (2)

R side (2)

S bottom

Q front/back (2)

B long framing (2)

F side wall (2)

G front/back wall (2)

C short framing (5)

D decking (2)

V stringers (2)

W riser (2)

X tread (2)

A support posts (6)

PLAYHOUSE • INCHES (MILLIMETERS)

REFERENCE	QUANTITY	PART	STOCK	THICKNESS	(mm)	WIDTH	(mm)	LENGTH	(mm)
A	6	support posts	4×4	3½	(89)	3½	(89)	14	(356)
B	2	long framing	2×4	1½	(38)	3½	(89)	120	(3048)
C	6	short framing	2×4	1½	(38)	3½	(89)	81	(2057)
D	2	decking	plywood	¾	(19)	48	(1219)	84	(2134)
E	1	decking	plywood	¾	(19)	24	(610)	84	(2134)
F	2	side walls	plywood	¾	(19)	48	(1219)	60	(1524)
G	2	front/back walls	plywood	¾	(19)	48	(1219)	84	(2134)
H	2	gable ends	plywood	¾	(19)	26	(660)	84	(2134)
J	4	corner posts	2×4	1½	(38)	3½	(89)	48	(1219)
K	9	rafters	2×4	1½	(38)	3½	(89)	60	(1524)
L	2	roof panels	plywood	¾	(19)	43	(1092)	72	(1829)
M	2	roof panels	plywood	¾	(19)	12	(305)	72	(1829)
N	1	galvanized roof cap	steel	¾	(19)	3½	(89)	72	(1829)
P	144	shingles	plywood	¼	(19)	6	(152)	11	(279)
Q	2	planter front/back	1×4	¾	(19)	3½	(89)	18	(457)
R	2	planter sides	1×4	¾	(19)	3½	(89)	4	(102)
S	1	planter bottom	1×4	¾	(19)	3½	(89)	16½	(419)
T	2	front trim at roof	plywood	¾	(19)	6	(152)	52	(1320)
U		window trim	1×4	¾	(19)	3½	(89)	18LF	(5.4LM)
V	2	step stringers	plywood	¾	(19)	10½	(267)	16	(406)
W	2	step risers	2×4	1½	(38)	3½	(89)	21	(533)
X	2	step treads	plywood	¾	(19)	8½	(216)	22	(559)

1   Once I decided on the dimensions of the deck, I built a simple 2×4 frame and nailed the corners together.

2   I cut and installed a row of 2×4s in the frame to act as floor joists. To make sure the whole thing was square, I measured across the diagonals and adjusted the frame until the measurements were equal.

3 **(ABOVE)** My site wasn't even close to level — this meant that I'd end up with corner posts of different heights to produce a level deck. I started with the corner that was the highest and install a post at an arbitrary height. I raised the frame about 6" off the ground in this spot.

4 **(RIGHT)** You can work out from the first corner in any direction you please. I placed a long (7') level across the back edge of the deck and raised the corner of the frame until the bubble was centered. I then marked the corner post at this height and cut it accordingly.

TIP I used a framing nailer to help speed up the construction process, but it isn't essential. If you don't have one, you can rent one for around $50/day, which should be plenty of time, as long as you have all the materials on hand. Then again, it isn't that many nails to put in by hand. It'll only take you an hour or so extra to do it the old-fashioned way. Or, you could just use screws. However you proceed, you'll want to use galvanized fasteners that are made for outdoor use.

5 **(ABOVE LEFT)** With the second corner post installed, the third and fourth are marked out in the same way. This process should create a perfectly level deck. It is also easy to add additional support posts at this time by just setting them in place and marking them at the appropriate heights. I also recommend securing the posts with either carriage bolts or galvanized fasteners that are available at any home store.

6 **(ABOVE RIGHT)** After re-checking the assembly for square by measuring diagonals once again, I cut the decking material to length and began nailing it in place. I used ¾" plywood. I used two full-width pieces and one ripped to 24" wide. You'll want to make sure that the edges of the plywood panels are fully supported.

7 The wall panels are ¾" plywood as well. I crosscut them with a circular saw and began setting them into place.

8 To join the panels together, I used a 2×4 that spanned the area from top to bottom. I then nailed to create a strong interface.

9 **(ABOVE)** I found that it was easiest for me to plan out the door and window placement by setting the panels into place. I had made a preliminary sketch on paper, but seeing the design come to life in actual size was much more meaningful. I pre-cut the window in the left wall before standing it into place.

10 **(RIGHT)** The plywood panels that fit below the front gable were a snap to layout and cut with a jigsaw. I allowed 30" for the door width, and made the panell to the right of the door 36" wide. For the gable, I measured the length of the panel (84") and the height that I wanted (2' seemed about right). Once the gable end was cut out, I held it temporarily in place and drew lines to extend the door cutout by 6". I wanted to make sure that an adult could comfortably walk in and out. Again, it helped a lot to see this in actual size to make sure I was getting it right.

A NOTE ON THIS CONSTRUCTION METHOD This is a very small structure (5'×7') in an area that receives very little snow and is sheltered from high winds, so I felt perfectly safe relying on the strength of the ¾" material to make this playhouse quite robust. Thorough nailing (place a nail every 6") is also essential to its structural integrity. Traditional shear-wall construction (meaning, 2×4s with OSB [Oriented Strand Board] or similar sheathing) would be a good way to beef things up if you foresee extreme weather to be an issue.

12 **(LEFT)** Rather than running in the traditional direction, these cross-rafters are laid out horizontally. I space them every 12" to make sure that the sheathing will be well-supported. This method simplifies the construction because there is no need to work out the math involved in laying out traditional rafters, and, it provides adequate strength for a small structure. If you live in a region where snow loads or other weather-related phenomena are significant, you may wish to beef this up somewhat.

11 The rear gable is just a duplicate of the front. For extra support across the seam where the gables and walls meet, I added ¾"-thick plywood plates.

13 This photo shows the importance of supporting the edges of each section of roof sheathing. I overhung the sheathing about 7" past the gable ends.

ROOFING MATERIALS

No playhouse is complete without a water-tight roof to protect the interior from the weather. Some people opt to match the roof of their home: this might mean using asphalt shingles, corrugated metal panels or cedar shakes. Being frugal (I like to use reclaimed materials whenever possible), I fabricated my own shingles out of scrap wood. With a heavy coat of finish, they'll hold up fine.

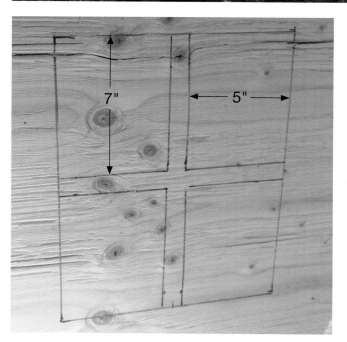

14 **(ABOVE)** The whole thing is shaping up nicely.

15 **(LEFT)** I decided to add a small window next to the front door. For ease of construction, I sketched the mullions on the plywood and cut around them with a jigsaw.

16 | Then I trimmed out the window with some scrap cedar.

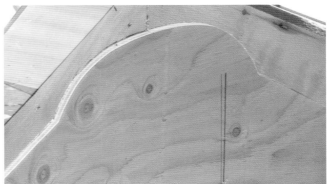

17 | I added some trim below the gable to jazz up the look. Just add your own creative touch.

18 | (LEFT) The large window was also trimmed out. I made this window fairly large because I wanted to have plenty of visual connection with the deck on that side.

19 | (ABOVE) A set of steps makes it easy for even small children to access the playhouse. I built the steps by cutting out a pair of risers and joining them with 2×4s, which provide plenty of stiffness. The steps are about 5½"-tall, as they are made to be walked on by short legs.

20 | I attached the steps by screwing them to the 2×4 that runs along the front of the deck.

FINISHING THE PLAYHOUSE I elected not to use exterior grade plywood, as it saved several hundred dollars. To ensure that the structure holds up over time, I made sure to finish it before it was exposed to rain or snow. I have no doubt that the finished product will easily last for a very long time. Make sure to choose a high quality exterior paint or stain and follow the manufacturer's instructions for best results.

For about $100 more, you could use Texture 111 (T-111), which is an exterior grade product that comes in 4×8 sheets. You've probably seen it, as it is commonly used for sheds and other similar applications. It is milled to look like individual boards, and it can be stained or painted.

TREEHOUSE 14

This project is guaranteed to bring out the "kid at heart" in anybody who builds one. I have great memories of playing in trees when I was young — an immense walnut in our backyard was a particular

favorite — and I've yearned for the chance to construct a tree house for the past few years now. While I had no illusions about reliving my youth —those days are past and gone — I was eager to build something that could help some of today's kids have a good time up amidst the leaves and branches. The opportunity eventually presented itself, and it has been a lot of fun for everyone.

Tree houses have enjoyed a bit of a resurgence in popularity over the past decade or so, and there are a handful of great books on the subject if you'd like to immerse yourself. This chapter doesn't claim to be an all-encompassing reference, but I do feel that it

does an effective job of documenting the process and problem-solving that I went through in this particular case. Due to the natural variation in the trees we have to work with, no two tree houses will be alike, anyway, so my major goal was to illustrate the kinds of approaches that might assist you in your own project. Tackling a treehouse, as you'll see in this chapter, is a great technical and creative challenge because there are no flat, level, or square reference points to guide you. Because of this, there is bound to be some head-scratching along the way. I hope you enjoy the unique challenge of this kind of project as much as I did.

TREEHOUSE • INCHES (MILLIMETERS)

REFERENCE	QUANTITY	PART	STOCK	THICKNESS	(mm)	WIDTH	(mm)	LENGTH	(mm)
A	1	support post	4×4	3½	(89)	3½	(89)	54	(1372)
B	2	rim boards	2×8	1½	(38)	7½	(191)	10'	(3.04m)
C	5	joists, with hangers	2×6	1½	(38)	5½	(140)	96	(2438)
D	2	decking	4×8	¾	(19)	48	(1219)	96	(2438)
E	4	upper story joists	2×6	1½	(38)	5½	(140)	96	(2438)
F	3	upper story handrails	1×3	¾	(19)	2½	(64)	96	(2438)
G	12	pickets	1×3	¾	(19)	2½	(64)	42	(1067)
H	2	ladder sides	2×6	1½	(38)	5½	(140)	84	(2134)
J	6	ladder steps	2×6	1½	(38)	5½	(140)	18	(457)
K	5	wall material	CDX plywood	¾	(19)	48	(1219)	96	(2438)
L	2	roofing	CDX plywood	¾	(19)	48	(1219)	96	(2438)

Your tree house project will most likely vary quite a bit from mine, so this supplies list is meant to give you an idea of what and how much of each material was required for my tree house.

SAFETY TIPS

I'll go out on a limb and state that building a tree house poses some unique dangers — once you've left terra firma, you'll need to be extra careful. These tips are mostly just common sense, but I think it is worth articulating them here nonetheless:

DON'T GO IT ALONE: Even if you're used to working by yourself, you may want to recruit some helpers for at least part of the process, especially for lifting heavy or awkward components into place.

DON'T BE A HERO: At some point during the process of building a tree house, it is likely that you'll be tempted to do something dicey — standing on a flimsy branch to drive in a screw, for example. Don't do it. Heed your intuition: if something seems dangerous, it probably is. Similarly, I found that I had to frequently remind myself to slow down and pay attention so that I didn't do anything foolish.

LADDERS ARE YOUR FRIEND: More than once I found myself straining to reach something that was a bit beyond my grasp, and fortunately I had the presence of mind to climb down and reposition a ladder so that I could work more safely.

1 If you're lucky enough to have a perfect tree, or a cluster of them in the right place, you can skip this step, but for many of us, adding a support post will provide the right structure for a tree house that is both larger and more stable than nature alone might allow for. The first step in properly installing the post is to dig a hole that is about two feet deep and one foot wide.

2 If the going is tough — where there are trees, there are roots, which can be tricky to work around — you can rent a power auger for about $30 or $40. If you have a number of other holes to dig, or if you can share the fee and the tool usage with a neighbor, this option is fast and easy.

3 I've become a fan of the newer fast-setting concrete that is available at most home centers. It only takes a couple of hours to set up and it doesn't require any mixing. Just dump it in the hole and add water.

4 **(ABOVE LEFT)** While I waited for the concrete to set up, I hauled in the rest of the materials and began working on the main platform. Since I was working alone, I tacked a few braces made from scrap plywood into place to hold up the 2×8 boards that were to be secured directly to the tree trunks.

5 **(ABOVE RIGHT)** These braces aren't permanent, so they don't need to be pretty.

6 **(RIGHT)** With one end of the 2×8 perched on the brace, the other end can be raised and lowered as needed to level it. If the level doesn't manage to stay put, I suggest using a bungee cord or tape to hold it in place.

7 **(LEFT)** Once the 2×8 was level, I supported it temporarily with a 2×6 that ran diagonally to the ground.

8 **(BOTTOM LEFT)** I used 6" lag bolts to secure the 2×8. The holes needed to be pre-drilled through the 2×8 and partway (an inch or so) into the tree. I began by using galvanized lag bolts but they were way to soft and I snapped them in half as soon as I applied any significant pressure to them, so I took a trip back to the hardware store for zinc plated ones.

9 **(BOTTOM RIGHT)** Be sure to use large washers so that the heads of the lag bolts don't bury themselves in the 2×8s. If you're lucky enough to have an impact driver, it will provide a fast way to sink the bolts. Or, you can do what I did, which was to use a cordless drill to sink the bolts about ¾" of the way, and then a ratchet and socket to finish them off.

10 I repeated this process on the other side of the tree and attached a second 2×8 level with the first one. They weren't exactly parallel, since our trees (and support post) weren't arranged in a perfect square, but that's half the fun of building a tree house — you work with what you've got.

11 Some of the tree house manuals that I consulted in researching this project use 2×4s for floor joists, but I suggest 2×6s, as they'll provide a lot more stability. I used galvanized joist hangers to hold them in place. Make sure their tops are flush with the 2×8s. Note that three tree trunks converge at the far end of the platform. I added more structure here later, but this shows the basic idea of how the platform was constructed.

12 Since I like to take kind of a "belt-and-suspenders" approach when it comes to projects where safety is an issue, I recommend providing additional support for the 2×6s by attaching them to the 2×8s with 3" screws. This is probably unnecessary, since the joist hangers are quite sturdy, but it offers some peace of mind.

13 | Since a tree house is often built for kids, getting them involved is almost inevitable. Depending on their ages and interest levels, they can handle a variety of jobs from start to finish.

14 | Installing the decking is most likely a one-person job, since it is hard to walk around on the platform while the joists are still exposed, but it is nice to have help handing up the sheets of ¾" plywood. This platform is hardly a perfect square, so the sheets didn't go on at right angles. My method is to set the sheets in place one at a time and make sure that they overlap halfway on the joists. This will allow the adjacent sheets to be supported on the same joists. Any excess that overhangs beyond the platform can quickly be trimmed off with a jigsaw.

15 | Trimming around the tree trunks is super fun, at least in my view. The easiest approach is to "sneak up" on a perfect fit. Begin by making a cutout that is wide enough to fit around the trunk, and don't worry too much about the depth. You'll be able to see how deep the cutout has to go when you test-fit it for the first time.

16 | Remove small amounts of material, pushing the sheet into place, and then seeing where you'll need to cut out more. This usually takes a few tries — as many as six or eight aren't unusual for me — but a nice fit can be achieved in the end. You will need to cut gaps that are an inch wide or more to allow for movement and growth. This opening is too tight and still needs to be enlarged.

17　Here's a rather complex set of scribes at the end of the platform. I began with the big one first, as it went deepest into the plywood, then the middle one, and finally the shallowest cut. You can see here that the deck panels went together a bit like a jigsaw puzzle.

18　The platform seen from the side. I drew pencil lines across the deck to indicate the position of the joists. I suggest screwing through the plywood and into the joists at 12" intervals. I put in screws every 6" along the perimeter of the platform.

20　This close-up shows a healthy penchant for overkill: I fastened the 2×6s to the tree itself and to each other whenever possible. 6" lag screws provide plenty of strength and peace of mind.

19　One unique attribute of this tree house is that it features two levels: a small "crow's nest" is a fun supplement to the main structure below. Building it wasn't too hard since I had already constructed the platform beneath it. This part of the process began with an analysis of how best to support the small upper platform. Fortunately I had four trees to work with, so I knew that I would be able to have plenty of places to secure 2×6s for the frame.

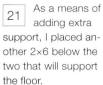

21 As a means of adding extra support, I placed another 2×6 below the two that will support the floor.

22 To help me figure out how and where to build the ladder, I placed a couple of 2×6s on an angle. This made it possible for me to envision the spacing required between the steps and the angle that they would need to be set to.

23 **(ABOVE)** The steps were secured with 4" screws and 6" lag bolts.

24 **(LEFT)** In a tree house, many joints won't be square. This makes for a fun and creative challenge.

25 The crow's nest is surrounded on all four sides by a sturdy railing with closely-spaced pickets. I put up the railings first.

26 The railings could take a beating over time, so I made sure they were very securely attached.

27 A level helped to make sure the pickets were plumb.

28 "Straight" and "flat" are two terms you might not use very often when building a tree-house.

29 When it came time to build walls for the lower platform, I worked backwards: rather than framing them with 2×2s or 2×4s, I put up sheets of plywood and then trimmed them as needed, then reinforced them with framing. I chose this approach because it was kind of hard for me to think about all of the odd angles and shapes that the walls would take. This method turned out to be easy and fast. (The cable in the foreground of the photo was for an unrelated project).

30 Because I was working alone, I found I could easily put the plywood sheathing up by resting its bottom edge on some supports that I tacked onto the main 2×8s and then screw the sheathing into the 2×8s.

31 The walls shaped up fairly quickly.

32 The roof needed enough of a slope to shed snow — an important consideration in our part of the country.

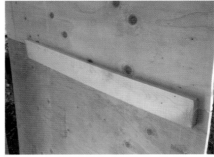

33 **(LEFT)** A jigsaw performed admirably at making door and window cutouts.

34 **(ABOVE)** Any butt joints between sheets of plywood needed to be reinforced from the inside.

35 **(ABOVE)** A couple of the sheets of plywood needed to be scribed to fit into place against pieces of framing. A compass traced the profile and outline of the material that will be removed.

36 **(RIGHT)** The finished product. This particular cut also creates a way of physically supporting the sheet of plywood by "hanging" it on the 2×6.

37 | The door is big enough for adults to use.

38 | A little bit of trim here and there dresses things up nicely.

39 | A sheet of plywood made a good workbench on which to assemble the ladder.

40 | A couple of the roof panels also needed to be scribed.

41 Putting on the roof was a bit tricky. I finally decided that the easiest approach was to place the plywood sheets on the roof and the trim them to fit. I used a straightedge to draw a line that followed the edge of the wall.

42 This was much easier than trying to figure out the exact sizes and angles and pre-cut them on the ground.

44 No tree house is complete without some look-out stations.

43 I used 2×4s to reinforce the walls on the inside.

RABBIT HUTCH

15

While I do not claim to be the world's foremost expert on housing rabbits, I do know a thing or two about it, and one of my strongest convictions is that there are a lot of uninspired rabbit hutches out there.

A quick Google search will pull up a lot of boring little boxes covered in wire mesh. Practical? Probably, but I couldn't resist jazzing things up a little. The end result sacrifices nothing in terms of functionality — the large doors provide easy access to clean out the whole interior, and the pitched roof will readily shed snow — the brightly colored sunshine motif below the eaves adds what I think is a bit of much-needed visual interest.

A structure like this would also make a fine home for a guinea pig or your choice of exotic birds (parrots, anyone?).

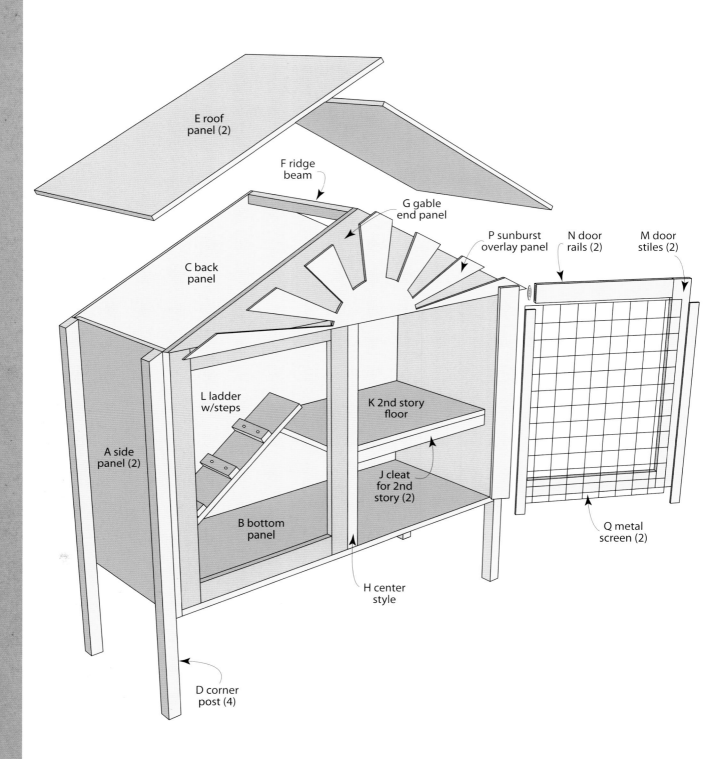

E roof
panel (2)

F ridge
beam

G gable
end panel

P sunburst
overlay panel

N door
rails (2)

M door
stiles (2)

C back
panel

L ladder
w/steps

K 2nd story
floor

A side
panel (2)

J cleat
for 2nd
story (2)

B bottom
panel

Q metal
screen (2)

H center
style

D corner
post (4)

RABBIT HUTCH • INCHES (MILLIMETERS)

REFERENCE	QUANTITY	PART	STOCK	THICKNESS	(mm)	WIDTH	(mm)	LENGTH	(mm)
A	2	side panels	plywood	3/4	(19)	18	(457)	30	(762)
B	1	bottom panel	plywood	3/4	(19)	18	(457)	48	(1219)
C	1	back panel	plywood	1/2	(13)	34	(864)	48	(1219)
D	4	corner posts	2×2	1 1/2	(38)	1 1/2	(38)	48	(1219)
E	2	roof panels	plywood	1/4	(6)	23	(584)	30	(762)
F	1	ridge beam	2×2	1 1/2	(38)	1 1/2	(38)	18	(457)
G	1	gable end panel	plywood	3/4	(19)	14	(356)	48	(1219)
H	1	center stile	2×2	1 1/2	(38)	1 1/2	(38)	40 1/2	(1029)
J	2	cleats for 2nd story	1×2	3/4	(19)	1 1/2	(38)	24	(610)
K	1	2nd story floor	plywood	3/4	(19)	16 1/2	(419)	24	(610)
L	1	ladder w/steps	plywood	1/2	(13)	6	(152)	24	(610)
M	4	door stiles	1×3	3/4	(19)	2 1/2	(64)	30	(762)
N	4	door rails	1×3	3/4	(19)	2 1/2	(64)	19	(483)
P	1	sunburst overlay panel	plywood	1/4	(6)	14	(356)	48	(1219)
Q	2	metal screen	galvanized			23	(584)	29	(737)
R	1	galvanized roof (or paint)				23	(584)	60	(1524)

1   The rabbit hutch starts out as a "U" shaped assembly made of 3/4"-thick plywood. The corners are screwed and glued together.

2   Instead of being a simple rectangle, the back must be cut to go all the way up to the roof line. Rather than get into a lot of complicated geometry here, I just held a tape measure out and decided that the peak of the roof looked about right at 14" above the sides, and then I transferred this measurement to the back panel by measuring up 14" at the center of the panel and drawing a pair of lines from this point to the tops of the sides. Thirty seconds of jig-sawing cut out the finished back.

3 **(LEFT)** To have some family bonding time, my wife helped out on this one, since she was as excited as I was about getting a rabbit. She screwed the back directly to the plywood with 1¼" screws at 6" intervals.

4 **(ABOVE)** The hutch is supported about a foot off of the ground on legs made from 2×2s. A clamp does a fine job of temporarily holding them in place.

5 **(ABOVE LEFT)** The legs are screwed to the hutch from the inside.

6 **(ABOVE RIGHT)** Once the legs are attached, the whole thing can be set upright, and it begins to look pretty good.

7 **(LEFT)** The tops of the legs must be trimmed so that the roof panels can sit down flush with the sides. To do this, use a straight-edge and extend the line of the roof from the back panel onto the legs, and trim the excess with a jigsaw.

8 | **(ABOVE)** To mark the front legs, I traced the cutoffs from the back legs, and this replicated the angle just fine.

9 | **(RIGHT)** With the legs trimmed properly, the roof panel can be set into place and tacked with brad nails into the tops of the 2×2s. The roof will require more support, but this is a good start.

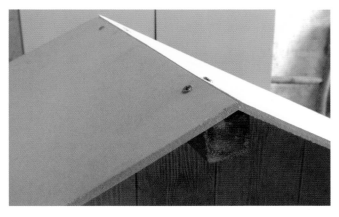

10 | I cut a small "ridge beam" from a scrap of 2×2 and screwed it into place where the two roof panels meet. This will ensure that the panels don't sag at the joint.

11 | The front of the roof is supported by a ¾"-thick plywood panel. I screwed it into place and then added additional reinforcement in the form of a vertical 2×2 (center stile) that runs behind it from the ridge to the floor of the hutch (visible in the next photo).

12 | This hutch has two levels so that its inhabitants will have the chance to run around and get some variety. The second level is supported by a pair of cleats that run horizontally.

13 | With the second level floor in place, I added a ramp.

14 The doors are made of simple rectangular frames which I biscuited together. You could also use dowels or pocket screws for an application like this. Mortise and tenon joints might be overkill here.

15 To cut the slots for the biscuits, I marked each joint with a small line that I could use to properly align my biscuit joiner.

16 (ABOVE LEFT) Once the doors were glued up, I clamped them and set them aside for a few hours. In the meantime, I turned my attention toward some aesthetic embellishments.

17 (ABOVE RIGHT) I knew from the beginning that I wanted to do some kind of fancy trim to dress up the hutch, and as the design evolved, it became more and more clear to me that the panel on the front right below the roofline would be the perfect spot. It occurred to me to create some kind of sunburst motif, and the next question was how to do so. I began by making a full-size drawing on some scrap cardboard.

18 (RIGHT) Once I had finished a drawing that I was happy with, I cut it out with an Xacto knife to create a one-piece pattern.

19 I traced the pattern onto a piece of ¼" plywood, and cut it out with a jigsaw. This resulted in a panel that could then be set into place like an onlay.

20 To simplify the painting process, I painted the sunburst onlay prior to attaching it to the hutch. At the same time, I painted the backdrop orange. Once both parts were dry, I glued and nailed the onlay to the backdrop. This method ensured that I didn't have to be at all fussy or careful in the painting, or do any touch-ups.

21 The wire mesh could be attached to the doors with staples, but I was concerned that they might eventually rust or fall out, so I secured the wire behind a set of strips that I screwed directly to the backs of the doors. From the front, the finished look is neat and clean, and I can rest assured that the wire won't come loose.

22 I wasn't expecting to house Houdini Hare, so I only used strips on the sides of the doors to attach the mesh.

23 A couple of simple strap hinges per door and a couple of latches, and the hutch is ready for occupancy.

CHICKEN COOP

16

Raising chickens is an old-school hobby that has seen a major resurgence over the past few years, and the trend seems to be just as popular in the city as it is in the country. My wife and I have had chickens for

about five years now, and this coop reflects some of what we've learned along the way. For example, this design features a parallel set of roosts: I've discovered that our hens like to cluster together tightly to stay warm on cold winter nights, and two roosts allows them to bunch up better than one. I've also discovered that our hens are happy to use a nesting box that is open at the top rather than the side, and this prevents eggs from rolling out and landing on the ground with a splat.

If you're not already on board, the popularity of small-scale chicken farming makes sense from many perspectives: number one on our list is that you'll quickly be hooked on the unbeatable taste of fresh eggs. And the price is friendly on your family's food budget — day-old chicks can be had for just a couple of dollars each, and they'll lay steadily for several years. Once your coop is built, they are as easy to care for as cats. Backyard chickens are also a lot of fun for adults and children alike — instead of watching TV, we've been known to sit around and watch the chickens once in a while. Our year-old daughter, in fact, makes a point of visiting with them at least twice a day.

From an environmental perspective, the benefits are pretty compelling, too — eating locally raised food is a common sense way to simplify without compromising on quality — and chickens will happily devour food scraps and kitchen waste. As a by-product, you'll receive top quality compost for gardening.

There are a lot of ways to house and manage chickens, and this chapter doesn't pretend to be a comprehensive guide. You'll find lots of free information on the topic on the internet. The dimensions you choose will naturally reflect the number of chickens that you plan to house: a structure of this size will provide ample roosting space for up to ten birds. And, while this is a versatile design that should work well in most parts of the country, you may wish to do some customizing to best suit the climate of your region.

If chickens aren't your thing, this design may still be useful to you or someone you

know: with a few easy modifications, this structure could do a fine job housing rabbits or guinea pigs, for example. Either way, this project provides a terrific opportunity to use up scrap wood: some projects require a large amount of material, but a chicken coop is made up of a lot of small parts, so you can use up whatever odds and ends you have lying around.

Before getting yourself outfitted to raise birds or any other animals, I recommend checking your local zoning codes to make sure that it is allowed. Our municipality allows up to 25 hens per property, but this will vary depending on where you live.

Fresh **EGGS**

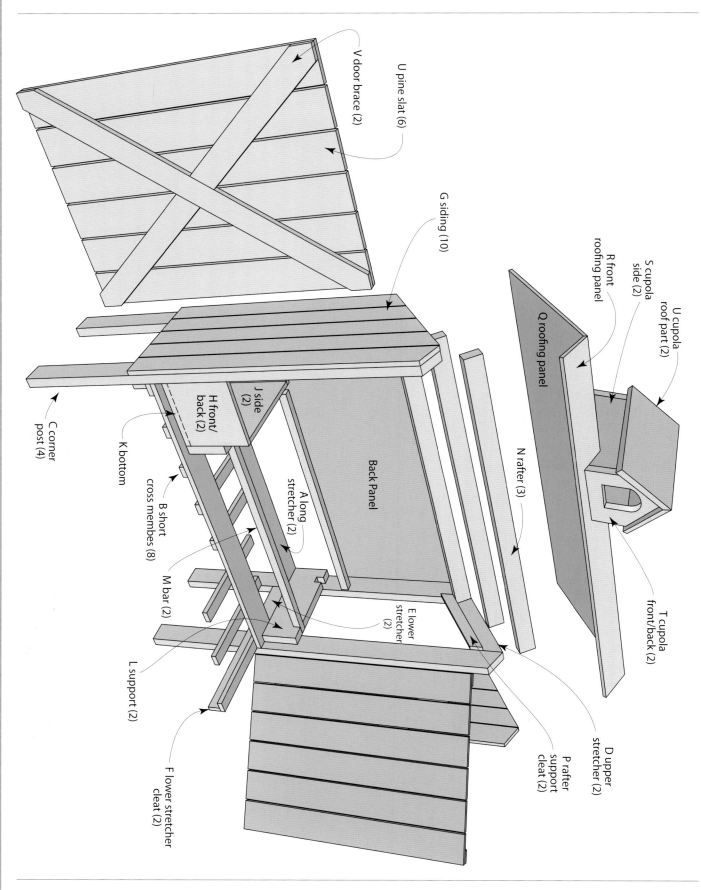

V door brace (2)

U pine slat (6)

G siding (10)

U cupola roof part (2)

S cupola side (2)

R front roofing panel

Q roofing panel

T cupola front/back (2)

N rafter (3)

C corner post (4)

K bottom

H front/back (2)

J side (2)

Back Panel

B short cross membes (8)

A long stretcher (2)

M bar (2)

E lower stretcher (2)

L support (2)

D upper stretcher (2)

P rafter support cleat (2)

F lower stretcher cleat (2)

CHICKEN COOP • INCHES (MILLIMETERS)

REFERENCE	QUANTITY	PART	STOCK	THICKNESS	(mm)	WIDTH	(mm)	LENGTH	(mm)
Bottom Subassembly									
A	2	long stretchers	1×6	3/4	(19)	5 1/2	(140)	54	(1372)
B	8	short cross-stretchers	1×2	3/4	(19)	1 1/2	(38)	18	(457)
Side Subassemblies									
C	4	corner posts	2×4	1 1/2	(38)	3 1/2	(89)	60	(1524)
D	2	upper stretchers	2×4	1 1/2	(38)	3 1/2	(89)	14	(356)
E	2	lower stretchers	2×4	1 1/2	(38)	3 1/2	(89)	11	(279)
F	2	lower stretchers cleat	1×4	3/4	(19)	3 1/2	(89)	18	(457)
G	10	siding	1×4	3/4	(19)	3 1/2	(89)	42	(1067)
	1	Back Panel	plywood	1/4	(6)	30	(762)	54	(1372)
Nest Box									
H	2	front/back panels	plywood	3/4	(19)	10	(254)	12	(305)
J	2	sides	plywood	3/4	(19)	10	(254)	15	(381)
K	1	bottom	plywood	3/4	(19)	10 1/2	(267)	15	(381)
Roosts									
L	2	supports	2×6	1 1/2	(38)	5 1/2	(140)	16	(406)
M	2	bars	2×2	1 1/2	(38)	1 1/2	(38)	42	(1067)
Roof									
N	3	rafters	1×4	3/4	(19)	3 1/2	(89)	54	(1372)
P	2	rafter support cleats	1×4	3/4	(19)	3 1/2	(89)	18	(457)
Q	1	roofing panel	plywood	3/4	(19)	20 1/4	(514)	60	(1524)
R	1	front roofing panel	plywood	3/4	(19)	5 1/2	(140)	60	(1524)
S	2	cupola sides	plywood	3/4	(19)	9	(229)	14	(356)
T	2	cupola front/back	plywood	3/4	(19)	9	(229)	14	(356)
U	2	cupola roof	roof parts	1/2	(13)	7 1/2	(191)	11 1/2	(292)
Doors									
V	12	pine slats	1×6	3/4	(19)	5 1/2	(140)	36	(914)
W	4	door braces	1×4	3/4	(19)	3 1/2	(89)	26	(660)

1 The floor of this coop is largely open so that night droppings accumulate below the coop and not in it. This will make for a cleaner coop and it also provides easy access to great fertilizer — the gardeners in your neighborhood will clamor for a chance to come and shovel it up. In the wintertime, it will be easy to just place a board across the opening to keep the coop warmer.

2 We tacked the slats in place with a nailer and then reinforced the joints with screws.

3 The sides of the coop feature a roof that slants toward the back so that snow will slide off and pile up in an out-of-the-way location. I didn't need to do any math to make these angled cuts: to begin, I just laid a straight-edged scrap at a "that-looks-about-right" angle and marked the line. Looking at the degree-finder on the miter saw showed me that I had selected a 25° angle.

4 (ABOVE LEFT) With the board placed against the rear fence of my miter saw, I simply swiveled the blade until it visually lined up with the mark. A shallow test cut proved that it was properly aligned.

5 (ABOVE RIGHT) To cut the stretchers that connect the two vertical pieces, I kept the saw at the same angle and cut one end of the stretcher. I then positioned the stretcher where it would eventually go and drew a pair of marks at the top and bottom edges of the stretcher where it intersected the rear vertical. I made sure that the vertical pieces were placed exactly parallel to each other at the correct width to ensure that these marks would be in the right spots. The marks showed me where to cut — I used my miter saw at the same 25° angle.

6 (RIGHT) Once the angled stretcher was cut, I drilled some holes for pocket screws.

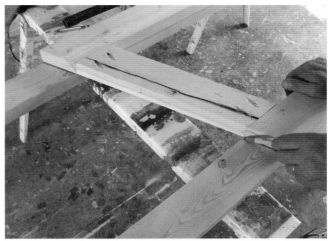

7 | The pocket hole screws provided a fast way of getting the sides assembled, and I reinforced them later on for additional strength.

8 | Once I had one side made, I laid it on top of a pair of 2×4s and traced it. This was faster than measuring the parts individually.

9 | The sides also required a horizontal stretcher about 20" up from the ground. I attached a cleat on the inside face of the side so that I would have somewhere to attach the coop's assembled bottom.

 10 | This photo shows how we nailed the bottom directly to the cleat. We reinforced this with 2" screws.

11 **(LEFT)** The project's skeleton shaped up rather quickly.

12 **(ABOVE)** Before standing up the frame, we decided to attach the back while it was still lying on the floor. This made it much easier to work with and it didn't risk damaging the wobbly sub-assembly. A structure such as this gets a great deal of its lateral stability when the back is attached. You'll notice that the back didn't extend all the way to the top: this is simply because we were working 100% with scrap wood on this project and we didn't have a large enough piece! We made up the difference with a smaller scrap and the finished result looked and worked fine.

13 The sides were made from scrap scavenged from a shipping pallet. We screwed them to the sides without cutting them to length beforehand to save time.

14 I transferred a mark around the sides to indicate the top and bottom of the angled side.

 15 **(ABOVE)** I connected the marks on the ends with a straight-edge and then cut it quite easily with a jigsaw.

16 **(RIGHT)** Cutting the boards all at once is much faster than cutting each board one-at-a-time, and it ensures a nice, even finished edge.

17 **(ABOVE)** My vision for the coop included a small decorative cupola (or should I say "coop-ola?"). This required that the roof come to a peak: I achieved this by cutting the front edge of the side panels with a jigsaw. Again, the angle didn't matter, so I didn't waste time laying it out too precisely: the goal was to make it look nice, and to cut both sides consistently.

18 **(RIGHT)** The nest box was made from scraps of 1×12s with a plywood bottom.

19 (ABOVE LEFT) A set of parallel roosts will allow the chickens to bunch up tightly to stay warm in cold weather or spread out on a hot night. The roosts were set into notches that I cut with a band saw on the edge of a scrap 1×6.

20 (ABOVE RIGHT) The roosts were made from some old 5/4 oak scraps that I made into octagonal shaped "dowels" with a chamfering bit on my router table. We pre-drilled holes and screwed them into the 1×6 supports on the ends so that the whole roost sub-assembly could be removed to be cleaned.

21 (RIGHT) I planned to use ¼"-thick scraps for the roofing material, and so I installed a set of 2"-thick plywood strips to make a row of rafters. These will provide plenty of strength when the snow flies next winter.

22 The rafters are supported by a cleat that follows the same angle as the roof.

23 I overlapped the ¼"-thick melamine panels that I used for the roof so that gravity would push snow off of the roof and not into the joint. Covering the roof with some galvanized tin sheeting would greatly enhance the roof's durability — I'll get to it before the weather turns!

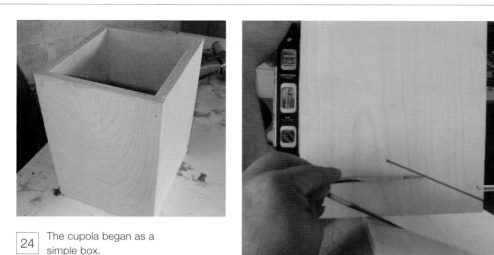

25 The bottom of the cupola had to be cut to fit on top of the roof — I used a level to hold it plumb and then used a pair of dividers to scribe a pair of lines that follow the roof's pitches (I used a red marker to make these lines stand out in the photos).

24 The cupola began as a simple box.

26 (ABOVE LEFT) Once I had cut one side of the cupola, I used an angle gauge to transfer these angles to the other side. This method works well and doesn't require any math.

27 (ABOVE RIGHT) If your jigsaw base will tilt, it'll make some of the cuts a bit easier.

28 (LEFT) The final fit was quite acceptable for a chicken coop. A little sanding cleaned up the tearout. The last step is the doors that, again, were made from scrap pallet material. I added interior braces across the width of the doors, and then added X bracing across the fronts for stabilty, strength and I think they look pretty nice, too.

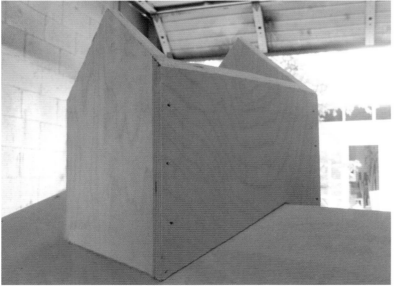

GRILLING STATION

17

We've all seen the high-end outdoor kitchens that have been touted as the ultimate in luxury on tv shows and in magazines, but these exotic beauties always come with a hefty price tag. The good news is that any moderately skilled homeowner can build and install a similar setup in a weekend for a fraction of the cost.

In terms of the functional aspects of the design, your options are pretty much endless. You could include a prep sink with hot and cold water, an integrated cutting board, an under-counter fridge, a wine cooler, and lots more. A bank of drawers might come in handy, and a wood-fired pizza oven might be nice, while you're at it.

In this chapter, I've decided to focus on the grilling station, since no outdoor kitchen is complete without it. Adapting the main concepts would be a pretty straightforward project. In terms of style, I went for a contemporary look that I thought would be at home in a variety of settings, but you could alter this to suit your own tastes. This design features a tile countertop that provides a lot of extra workspace, and the cabinets add a lot of storage to an area that formerly had none at all. The trickiest part is integrating the grill, so when I went grill-shopping, I made sure to buy a model that looked like it could be taken apart easily. With a little head-scratching and a little elbow grease, I'm sure that you could find a way to make nearly any grill work. If you don't mind less of a built-in look, the grill may simply be free-standing, (on its manufacturer-supplied base) between a pair of cabinets — this is certainly the easiest option.

In terms of grills, you can get more bang for your buck these days than ever before. A recent trip to a local home center brought me up to speed on the options — stainless steel, it appears, is hot these days, but my wife and I opted for a less-expensive (around $140) model that I was pretty sure we could dress up nicely. So far it has worked great: we like having the side-burner, and it has a much larger grilling capacity than our old one. The side burner is a really handy feature that, once you get used to, is hard to live without. Making it work in the new grill center was a challenge, however, due to the way that it was constructed. More on that later.

The overall size of the finished product will naturally be determined by your own personal criteria, but it is worth mentioning that, even though I built an in-line configuration, an "L" shaped unit could look great if you have the space. You might even want to integrate a bar-height counter with seating.

And while I didn't get into it here, you might also consider using stone veneers, available at your local home improvement store. They're easy to work with, and will lend the beauty of custom stone work to your outdoor kitchen.

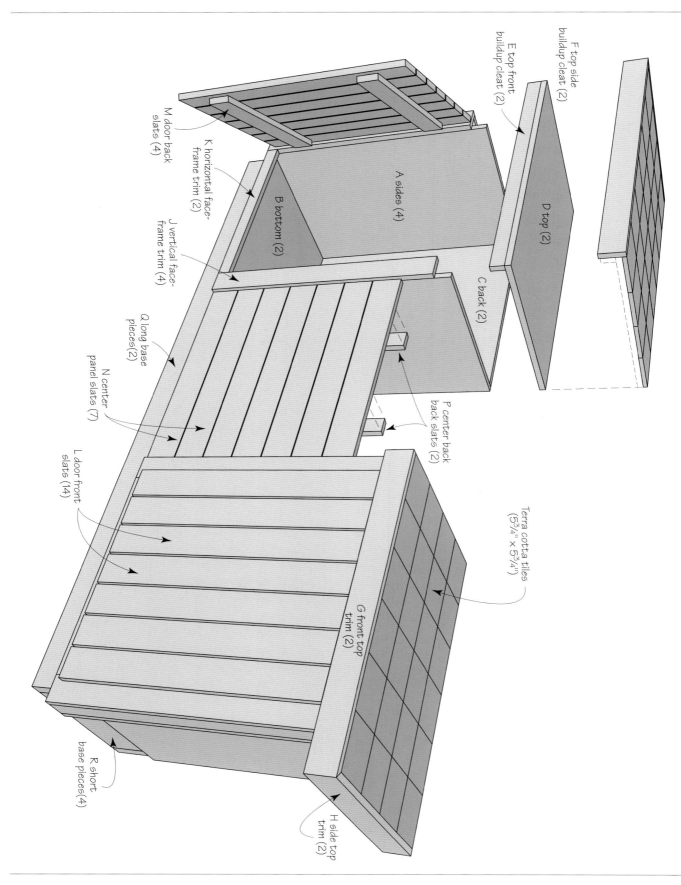

F top side
buildup cleat (2)

E top front
buildup cleat (2)

M door back
slats (4)

K horizontal face-
frame trim (2)

J vertical face-
frame trim (4)

B bottom (2)

A sides (4)

D top (2)

C back (2)

Q long base
pieces(2)

N center
panel slats (7)

P center back
back slats (2)

L door front
slats (14)

Terra cotta tiles
(5³/₄" × 5³/₄")

G front top
trim (2)

R short
base pieces(4)

H side top
trim (2)

GRILLING STATION • INCHES (MILLIMETERS)

REFERENCE	QUANTITY	PART	STOCK	THICKNESS	(mm)	WIDTH	(mm)	LENGTH	(mm)
Cabinets									
A	4	Sides	plywood	3/4	19	21 3/4	552	31	787
B	2	Bottoms	plywood	3/4	19	21	533	27	686
C	2	Backs	plywood	3/4	19	27	686	31	787
D	2	Tops	plywood	3/4	19	23	584	35	889
E	2	Front build-up cleats	pine/poplar	3/4	19	1 1/2	38	35	889
F	2	Side build-up cleats	pine/poplar	3/4	19	1 1/2	38	22 1/4	565
G	2	Front top trims	cedar	3/4	19	3	76	35 3/4	908
H	2	Side top trims	cedar	3/4	19	3	76	23	584
J	4	Vertical face frames	cedar	3/4	19	3	76	29 1/2	750
	2	Vertical face frames	cedar	3/4	19	2 1/4	57	29 1/2	750
	2	Vertical face frames	cedar	3/4	19	1 1/2	38	29 1/2	750
K	2	Horizontal face frame	cedar	3/4	19	1 1/2	38	24 3/4	629
Doors/Front Panel									
L	14	Door front slats	pine	3/4	19	4	102	29	737
M	2	Door back slats	pine	3/4	19	3	76	24	610
N	7	Center panel slats	pine	3/4	19	4	102	27 1/2*	679
P	2	Center panel back slats	pine	3/4	19	3	76	28	711
Base									
Q	2	Long pieces	pine	1 1/2	38	3 1/2	89	84 1/2*	2147
R	4	Short pieces	pine	1 1/2	38	3 1/2	89	14 3/4*	375

* Adjust size to fit your grill.

1 In planning the grilling station, it pays to choose a suitable grill; this model features "wings" on the sides that can be easily unbolted, and this will make it easier to integrate the unit into the shop-built portions of the project.

2 The entire assembly will be perched on a solid base that can be easily shimmed and leveled on any spot. This chapter illustrates how I built an in-line design, but you could just as easily construct an "L"-shaped one.

3 The cabinets start out as simple, plywood "U" shapes. The bottoms and backs are screwed between the sides, with the backs also screwed to the back edge of the bases.

4 The cabinets are the same size, and I set their outward-facing sides flush with the sides of the base.

5 I made sure that the 2x4's that connect the front and back part of the base were located where they would be able to support the grill.

6 I needed to notch one of the cabinets so that the hose could run to the burners. There was no harm in making an extra-large notch, and it guaranteed that I'd be able to line things up later on.

7 I ripped cedar 1x4's into a couple of different widths, and using glue and brad nails, I assembled a couple of square columns that I then fastened to the front of the cabinets. This trim was purely decorative in nature, as the cabinets were strong enough on their own.

8 I placed the columns on the far ends of the unit and trimmed the front edges to match with cedar.

9 You could join the pieces of cedar trim with pocket screws (the result would be a face-frame, basically), or you could simply glue and nail the pieces into place.

10 I cut the tops to size to test their fit. I wanted no overhang at all on the inside edges of the cabinets so that the grill could drop in and fit tightly, but I liked the look of an overhang at the sides. Also, my cedar trim was held shy in height, as the countertops will receive a thicker edge that will fill the gap.

11 I found some great 6x6 terra cotta tiles at our local home center, and I laid them out on the sub-top just to make sure they fit. Good thing I did — it turned out that I needed to trim a bit off the edge of the tops.

12 Now that the subtop has been built-out, the gap at the top of the cedar trim is a non-issue. The beefy countertop also a better finished look, too.

14 The left-hand wing came off easily. The right one would prove a bit trickier, as it had a separate burner attached. More on this later.

13 One of the things I like about this project is the contrast between the cedar trim and the pine door panels. The doors are constructed quite simply with battens across the back. I used tapered dowels to maintain a uniform gap between the boards. A clamp kept the parts from shifting during assembly.

15 **(LEFT)** Once I removed the wheels and casters, I set the grill into place. The left side needed to be shimmed up to level the grill.

16 **(BELOW LEFT)** The left-hand cabinet dropped right into place.

17 **(BELOW RIGHT)** I screwed the cabinet directly into the metal frame of the grill. This was not only very strong, but it helped to lock the two components together tightly.

18 **(LEFT)** Although this project is pretty straightforward, it does require you to connect and disconnect some gas fittings, so use caution and take your time hooking things up.

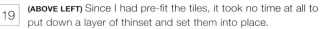

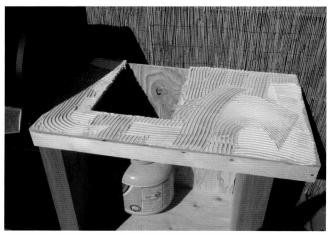

19 (ABOVE LEFT) Since I had pre-fit the tiles, it took no time at all to put down a layer of thinset and set them into place.

20 (ABOVE RIGHT) I decided to set the burner into the tile counter-top on the right-hand side of the grill. This required me to lay out the tiles accordingly to ensure a good fit.

21 (RIGHT) Once I cut out the required hole with a jigsaw, I tiled the right-hand side of the grill.

22 (BELOW) I had to get creative and cut the burner out of the factory-made wing, but it eventually worked out great.

23   **(ABOVE)** The edges of the countertop were trimmed out in cedar, too.

24   **(LEFT)** The center panel of the grill was covered up with a panel that mimicks the door style. For variety, I decided to spin the orientation of the boards 90 degrees. Six magnetic catches hold the panel in place, but leave removal easy.

25   **(BOTTOM LEFT)** The side burner has a separate control knob which required a cut-out on the front of the countertop. You'll also notice that I relocated the propane tank to the interior of this cabinet for easy access.

26   **(BOTTOM RIGHT)** Once the knob was installed, the whole thing had a neat and clean look to it.

RUSTIC FURNITURE 18

This genre of furniture is really perfect for anyone, from beginner to expert. Beginners will be able to craft a useful item that requires minimal tools and experience, experts will enjoy seeing a project come together

quickly and may wish to improvise with more complicated designs.

In terms of crafting the required joinery, I used a round tenon cutter that mounts in a hand-held drill. The cutter isn't cheap, but it is the fastest way I've found to make rustic looking joints that really hold up. If you're only making one piece, it may be hard to justify the investment in the tool, but for larger pieces (or multiples), the tool starts earning its keep pretty quickly. You might also be able to justify the investment by considering that the actual materials are most likely going to be free. In my case, a storm came through

and took out a ton of branches in our neighborhood. In about ten minutes, I'd easily rounded up a pile of perfect specimens, and the neighbors were only too happy to have me haul them away. I even got into the habit of carrying around a handsaw in the trunk of my car so that I could quickly cut down branches that I discovered in the course of my daily travels.

In addition to saving you money on materials, this type of furniture also won't require much in the way of sophisticated tooling. Table saw, routers, and dovetail jigs won't help you here- a drill and a saw are all you need. Pretty

much all the cuts you'll need to make can be accomplished with a jigsaw, a chop saw, or even handsaw. Frankly, you won't even need a shop — this is back-porch woodworking at its finest.

In terms of materials, I don't worry specifically about the exact parts ahead of time — I just make sure that I have enough parts of the right orders of magnitude — that is to say, before I start a chair, I make sure to have a few long, thick pieces for the rear legs, and a bunch of smaller-diameter pieces which can be used as stretchers. Once I'm back at the shop, I can sort through the pile more closely and pick out pieces that match best in terms of shape and size. When in doubt, having a few extras to begin with is the way to go.

An inherent trait to this type of woodworking is that it doesn't limit you to right-angle designs. Branches are

anything but straight, so this is an opportunity to incorporate the character of the material as you find it. Playful asymmetry is one of the defining characteristics of this style — imposing too much rigidity or exactness is kind of missing the point, in my view.

You have two basic choices when working with non-standard materials such as these — you can either follow the constraints that the materials impose, or you can work in such a way as to minimize the effects of these properties. For example, I started out assuming that the rear legs of this chair would be parallel (perpendicular to the ground), similar to the familiar ladder-back style of chair. Once I began to assemble the parts, however, it became clear that the unique curves of the rear legs — which were the attribute that drew me to

these pieces in the first place — weren't really going to cooperate. They seemed best-suited to a configuration where the rear legs tapered towards each other from bottom to top. My choice, then was to go with the flow or to discard one or both of the legs and find others that would remain true to my original design idea. I chose the former, but this is just a personal preference. Some parts really do need to be set aside from time to time, as they truly can be unsuitable for a particular application.

In any event, you'll keep your sanity if you learn to break the process down and work in terms of sub-assemblies. Because the materials can throw you a curveball, I've found it easier to proceed one step at a time rather than trying to put everything together at once and risk having things go together sloppily

(or worse, not at all). As an example, the most obvious place to start with a chair is the rear leg assembly, then a separate front leg assembly, then join the two halves with side stretchers. It helps to be ready to make adjustments along the way — for instance, I had cut a set of stretchers of equal length, which would've been fine on a "normal" furniture project that used flat, square, and straight lumber. Working with unprocessed materials, however, means that a lot of the rules of thumb that I've picked up over the years don't apply. I ended up only using half of the stretchers that I'd pre-cut, and I needed to make longer ones to fit the rest. I also recommend dry fitting parts prior to glue-up because it gives you a chance to make adjustments.

RUSTIC SIDE CHAIR

1 | For a chair, I like to start by selecting a couple of larger pieces for the back legs. They don't have to match exactly, but it helps if they are similar in their overall shape (i.e. straight-up or slightly curved, etc.)

2 | I find it much easier and more effective to organize the project into a few sub-assemblies that will later be put together to form the entire piece. In this case, I began by marking out locations for the horizontal stretchers that will complete the rear leg and back assembly of the chair. A marker shows up well on the bark.

3 | (LEFT) I find it handy to also layout the holes that will receive the side stretchers at this point. It isn't necessary, but helps me to smooth out the workflow by thinking ahead just a bit.

4 | (ABOVE) A forstner or spade bit works fine to quickly bore holes in the green lumber.

TENON CUTTER 101 The cutters (mine, at least) offers a slight degree of adjustability which allows some variety in the size of the tenons it cuts. I recommend doing a couple of test joints on scrap the first time you use the tool, so that you can be sure that you correctly match the drill bit to fit the tenons. For example, my ¾" cutter cuts tenons from ⅝" to ⅞", so assuming a ¾" drill bit will cut a suitable tenon introduces a lot of room for error, which could translate to loose joints that will fail in time.

5 **(ABOVE)** Cutting the round tenons is a snap with a dedicated cutter. At around $100 (www.leevalley.com), they aren't cheap, but they quickly pay for themselves if you make a couple of pieces of furniture. Their efficiency is unbeatable. Make sure to clamp the workpiece firmly for safety's sake. If you haven't used a cutter like this before, I suggest testing it out on some scrap to get a feel for it. You'll quickly master it.

6 **(RIGHT)** The completed rear assembly.

7 Once the glue has dried in the rear assembly, I stood it up and began to plan out the rest of the chair. I chose a couple of pieces for the front legs and spaced them out as necessary.

8 **(ABOVE)** This is the completed front sub-assembly, which was constructed in the same manner as the rear one.

9 **(RIGHT)** While I waited for the glue to dry on the front assembly, I selected four side stretchers, cut them to length, and milled tenons on their ends. The clamp serves to hold the whole thing together temporarily.

11 Once the holes have been drilled for the side stretchers, the entire chair can be glued up and clamped. I like to use polyurethane glue for this purpose because it is both strong and weather-resistant.

10 To mark the location of the holes, I clamp the parts in place and trace the tenons with a marker. In this photo, I've pulled the stretcher aside for clarity.

12 **(ABOVE LEFT)** This is the entire arsenal of tools required for a project like this. Who needs a shop? A jointer or planer will just gather dust when you're building rustic furniture in this style.

13 **(ABOVE RIGHT)** I've experimented with some different materials on seats and backs — here is one of my first attempts at a loosely-woven seat. I was going for a rough-and-ready look, and that's what I ended up with, all right! The result is quite strong, despite its rag-tag appearance. A much more refined aesthetic could be achieved with a bit more time, patience, and know-how.

14 **(RIGHT)** I've also had success in using old reclaimed planks for seats and backs. They certainly are fast to build and attach — I secure them with screws.

RUSTIC ARMCHAIR

1 Construction on this arm chair follows the same pattern as outlined in the previous project. I did vary slightly, deciding to bring the round tenons all the way through. This photo shows a tenon prior to having the excess glue wiped off — you'll want to take care of this before the glue sets, because you can't really sand off any dried glue at the risk of destroying the bark.

2 The arms on this chair were formed from solid wood blanks (2x4's, actually). To create a nice fit between the end of the 2x4 and the irregular curve of the tree branch that it will abut, I used a compass. This will neatly scribe the profile onto the wood and indicate the portion that needs to be removed.

3 (ABOVE LEFT) Once the joint at the back has been cut, the rest of the arm can be shaped to your tastes. The arm on the left shows the result after a fair amount of shaping. To make the required cuts, I used a jigsaw with the base angled where needed.

4 (ABOVE RIGHT) The joint at the back should be pinned with a long screw.

5 (RIGHT) Because the back leg slanted a bit, I had to cut the edge of the arm at an angle to correspond. This was done by setting the base of the jig saw at an angle that I judged by eye.

RUSTIC SIDE TABLE

1 **(LEFT)** I liked the fact that a couple of the branches were forked at one end, so I decided to go with the asymmetry.

2 **(BELOW LEFT)** Once the glue had dried, I was able to join the two sides together with a pair of long stretchers. Two clamps were all I needed to maintain adequate pressure.

3 **(BELOW RIGHT)** I used a board of rough-sawn mulberry for the bottom shelf. A few years ago, I lucked into a nice little stack of mulberry lumber that came from a tree just a few miles from my shop. The branches also came from the neighborhood, which is kind of neat.

4 **(LEFT)** The top is also made of mulberry.

Protecting wood from the ravages of the elements is a tall order. It certainly can be done, and I'll recommend a couple of specific products that have a good track record, but first let me present what might be best called an inconvenient truth:

Every outdoor finish should be viewed
as a temporary solution.

While I would love to be able to point toward a particular product or process that provides perfect results and lasts forever, such a magic solution just doesn't exist. So, be forewarned: finishes that are exposed to the elements will have to be periodically maintained, and if they aren't, the finishes will eventually fail and look pretty crummy.

The main culprits are the twin demons of Ultraviolet spectrum light (UV) and moisture, and it often appears that the former creates just as much havoc as the latter. It's perhaps natural to assume that water poses a greater threat, but the opposite is often true: long exposure to sunlight — particularly at high altitudes — can be a finish's worst enemy. I know professional finishers who will turn down a project based on the amount of sunlight that the project will be exposed to, as they realize they're going to be called back after a short time to begin fighting an uphill battle.

So, with this in mind, I'd like to present a second option: embracing weathering as a natural process that can look nice in its own right. This won't work for every project, but if you like the look of outdoor furniture with "character", then this choice may be right for you. Beware, however, that this approach is best reserved for certain rot-resistant woods, and softer materials like pine and fir will probably deteriorate more quickly than you'd like if left unprotected.

So, the starting point in the quest to properly finish wood for the great outdoors has to begin by examining your expectations. Are you prepared to maintain (meaning scuff-sand and recoat) the finish every few years? Even the best finish will need attention every two-to-five years. Do you expect a refined finish that is similar to indoor furniture? If so, you'll need to apply a lot of coats to begin with, and you'll pay accordingly for a high-end finishing product. Or are you thinking about a more rustic project that will be allowed to age gracefully? These questions will help guide you to the right solution for your needs.

If you have some background with wood finishes, you're aware that most products come in one of two categories: penetrating oils; or film finishes. The names are apt descriptors. Penetrating oils, often tinted with stain, sink into the pores of the wood and are an effective way of changing wood's natural color. They are tempting because they're so easy to apply — just flood the surface and then wipe away the excess. Unfortunately, this ease of application comes at a price: they offer almost nothing in terms of protection against nature. Yes, they look good on day one, but over the course of even a single year, they offer basically no advantages to just doing nothing. Wood will tend to weather just as much as if it had been completely untreated.

Film finishes include varnishes, polyurethanes and lacquers. To hold up outdoors, many people turn to spar varnishes, with mixed results. They generally require at least four coats, and will probably need to be maintained yearly, depending on the weather in your area. I've had some poor results with spar varnish on some projects in my own backyard, but I probably needed a thicker buildup of the product — I did three coats on a small tabletop, and it had flaked off completely in less than a year. Or perhaps the surface wasn't clean enough to begin with, so the new finish never properly adhered to the wood.

Epifanes was recently rated the best in comparison by a major woodworking magazine. Although the product was originally designed for use on wooden boats, it will hold up just fine on furniture and other outdoor woodwork. Beware, however, that simply choosing the best-rated product doesn't mean that the process will be easy: the manufacturer recommends six coats, which will take a while, since you'll need to allow a day between coats.

Another approach that I've heard great things about is the Cetol system from Sikkens. It's a two-part system in that it recommends you use Cetol 1 as a base coat, and then two coats of Cetol 23 as a top coat. Three coats sound better than the six suggested for the Epifanes, and the cost is comparable between the two products.

If you don't mind stepping away from wood tones, paint is always a good option, and oil-based paints will hold up much better than later ones. I recommend using a semi-gloss finish so that the final surface will be easy to clean, and you'll want to take the time to apply a coat of exterior-rated primer first. I also suggest that the paint you choose is rated highly for color retention — not all exterior paints are created equal in this regard, and I've seen some that faded quite noticeably in just a couple of years.

What about deck stains? Nope. I've actually tried this approach with a set of dining chairs that I made for my own home four years ago. The stain colored the wood in a pleasing way, which was certainly one of my objectives, but the resulting finish was rough and not quite appropriate for furniture. It held up fine for a couple of years, and then it clearly needed another coat, because it had faded quite a bit and looked rather tired. It's worth mentioning, however, that the color at least remained uniform — that is to say, there was no peeling, streaking or chipping in the finish. My conclusion was that deck stains certainly have their role: for something like a fence, deck or shed, they are a good solution.

DESIGNING FOR THE GREAT OUTDOORS

If you're used to building furniture for the great indoors, you'll need to do a few things differently when it comes to projects that can withstand the wear and tear that the elements will impose. One of the most notable areas to pay attention to is in fastener selection — ordinary zinc-coated screws and bolts simply won't hold up outside. They'll rust and eventually fail. For this reason, I recommend fasteners made from stainless steel, or ones that are at least coated suitably to stand up to moisture.

You may also want to choose materials that have a well-known track record for holding up agains the elements. While all of the species on the list below might not be available in your area, most people should have access to at least a few:

DECAY-RESISTANT SPECIES
    Cedar
    Cherrry (black)
    Chestnut
    Cypress (Arizona)
    Ipe
    Juniper
    Locust (black)
    Mahogany
    Mesquite
    Mulberry (red)
    Oak (bur, chestnut Gambel, Oregon white, post and white)
    Osage-orange
    Redwood
    Sassafras
    Walnut (black)
    Yew (Pacific)

Another area that merits some special attenion is the wide world of adhesives. For outdoor projects, I've used the following with good results:

- Polyurethane-type adhesives (Gorilla Glue)
- Titebond II and Titebond III
- Epoxy
- Construction adhesive

Every adhesive has its pros and cons. Here's a short list of tips that may help out:

Polyurethane glue will tend to produce a lot of foamy squeeze-out. This residue will have to be removed and I suggest using a wet sponge while the product is still wet. It also scrapes off easily with a chisel once it's dry.

When using polyurethane glue, if you get any glue on your hands, make sure to wash them throroughly while the glue is still wet — otherwise it'll have to wear off, and this can take a long time!

Construction adhesives can be a poor choice for precisely-fit joinery, but a very good solution for applications where gap-filling strength is advantageous.

The performance of all adhesives can be improved by increasing the amount of gluing surface. One way to do this is to use lapped joints.

IDEAS. INSTRUCTION. INSPIRATION.

THESE AND OTHER GREAT **POPULAR WOODWORKING** PRODUCTS ARE AVAILABLE AT YOUR LOCAL BOOKSTORE, WOODWORKING STORE OR ONLINE SUPPLIER.

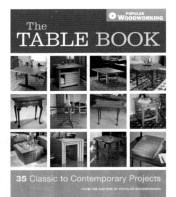

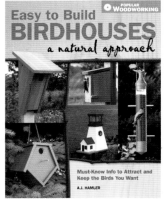

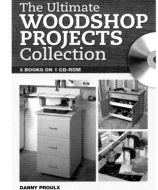

THE TABLE BOOK
FROM THE EDITORS OF POPULAR WOODWORKING
You'll find a table in every woodworking style to fit your needs and individual tastes. And, while building the projects, your woodworking skills will be challenged and improved!

ISBN 13: 978-1-4403-0427-9
paperback • 272 pages • Z7128

EASY TO BUILD BIRDHOUSES
BY A.J. HAMLER
Projects range from traditional designs to a lighthouse, a cottage and a football helmet and more! Fun to build and fun to watch the birds move into their new home!

ISBN 13: 978-1-4403-0220-6
paperback • 144 pages • Z5979

POPULAR WOODWORKING MAGAZINE
Whether learning a new hobby or perfecting your craft, *Popular Woodworking Magazine* has expert information to teach the skill, not just the project. Find the latest issue on newsstands, or order online at www.popularwoodworking.com.

THE ULTIMATE WOODSHOP PROJECT COLLECTION
CD-ROM, BOOKS BY DANNY PROULX
This CD-ROM gives you all the information you need to make your shop the best it can be.

ISBN 13: 978-1-4403-0241-1
This disc includes the full book content from: *Building Woodshop Workstations, Toolboxes & Wookbenches* and *50 Jigs & Fixtures.*
CD-ROM • Z6474

Visit **www.popularwoodworking.com** to see more woodworking information by the experts.

Recent Articles

Read the five most recent articles from Popular Woodworking Books.

• **Kitchen Makeovers - Pull-Out Pantry Design & Construction**
• **Woodshop Lust Tom Rosati's Woodshop**
• **Woodshop Lust David Thiel's Woodshop**
• **Wood Finishing Simplified Strictly, Stickley Oak**
• **Wood Finishing Simplified In a Pickle (Whitewash on Oak or Pine)**

Featured Product

Made By Hand
$21.95

MADE BY HAND

Made By Hand takes you right to the bench and shows you how to start building furniture using hand tools. By working through the six projects in this book, you'll learn the basics of hand-tool woodworking and how to use the tools effectively and efficiently, then add joinery skills and design complexity. The accompanying DVD includes valuable insight into the tools themselves and a look at the techniques that make these tools work so well.

Note from the Editor

Welcome to Books & More
We've got the latest reviews and free sample excerpts from our favorite woodworking books, plus news on the newest releases. Check out the savings at our Woodworker's Book Shop, and don't miss out on building your Wish List for the holidays. If you missed our newsletter's **"Print Is Dead"** poll results, check them here, and subscribe (below) to our newsletter to receive special sale items and book reviews not found anywhere else.

– *David Baker-Thiel, Executive Editor Popular Woodworking Books*

A woodworking education can come in many forms, including books, magazines, videos and community feedback. At Popular Woodworking we've got them all. Visit our website at www.popularwoodworking.com to follow our blogs, read about the newest tools and books and join our community. We want to know what you're building.

Sign up to receive our weekly newsletter at http://popularwoodworking.com/newsletters/